TORAH AND THE NEW COVENANT

An Introduction

Daniel Gruber

Elijah Publishing
PO Box 776
Hanover, NH 03755

ISBN 0-9669253-0-0

TABLE OF CONTENTS

INTRODUCTION

In the ancient city of Derbent in the Caucasus, there were two synagogues facing each other on opposite sides of the same street. Traditionally in a synagogue, there is one wall which signifies the direction in which the worshippers should pray, facing towards Jerusalem. The communities which established the two synagogues originally came from different places in the Diaspora, one from the east and one from the west.

As each community travelled and settled in new locations, they preserved the orientation towards Jerusalem of the original place from which they had started. That is what they did when they arrived in Derbent. In the same town, on the same street, their synagogues pointed in opposite directions to Jerusalem.

That is the way it is with the Church and the Synagogue. Some shifting here, some shifting there, and two communities which both started out long ago from Jerusalem, now point their members in opposite directions to pray and serve God.

Many people, great theologians among them, have seen an irreconcilable conflict between Torah, i.e. the Law of Moses, and the New Covenant which Yeshua (Jesus) brought. Consequently they see two very different religions presented in the Bible — one Jewish, the other Christian. History, at least from the fourth century on, certainly seems to affirm their perspective.

Such history, however, does not actually establish what is true and what is false. It merely demonstrates what people, centuries after the fact, have chosen to accept as true and false. Such history is simply the record of how those choices have been acted out.

If Truth is determined by human decrees and actions, then the issue is already settled. There is no need to discuss what both the Church and the Synagogue have agreed upon, though in opposition to each other, for many, many centuries.

On the other hand, if human decrees and actions are engraved not in stone but upon the shifting sands of time, then Truth may well be different from what everyone already knows and has agreed upon. Truth may even exist apart from man, unchangeable no matter what anyone says, does, or knows.

If that is so, then it becomes legitimate to question and challenge what everyone affirms as unquestionable. It becomes legitimate to examine the Scriptures anew in the hope of distinguishing between ageless wisdom and accumulated error. That is the purpose of this introductory examination of the Biblical teaching concerning Torah and the New Covenant.

I have not found the irreconcilable conflict that others have. I have found instead a consistent God, ruling over all. That consistent God has always sought justice and righteousness. That is why He gave His Law to Israel. (cf. Is.5:1-7)

That is why keeping His Law is equated with loving Him. "Be very careful to keep the commandment and the law that Moses the servant of the LORD gave you: to love the LORD your God, to walk in all His ways, to obey His commandments, to hold fast to Him and to serve Him with all your heart and all your soul." (Josh. 22:5)

That is why, "The LORD warned Israel and Judah through all His prophets and seers: 'Turn from your evil ways. Observe My commandments and decrees, in accordance with the entire Law that I commanded your fathers to obey and that I delivered to you through My servants the prophets.' " (2Kgs. 17:13)

It was disobedience to God's Law that constituted Israel's sin. "They made their hearts as hard as flint and would not listen to the law or to the words that the LORD Almighty had sent by His Spirit through the earlier prophets. So the LORD Almighty was very angry." (Zech. 7:12)

The two great commandments in the Law of Moses are: "Hear O Israel, the Lord our God, the Lord is one. And you shall love the Lord your God with all your heart, with all your soul, and with all your might." (Dt.6:4-5) "...and you shall love your neighbor as yourself." (Lev.19:18 cf. Mk.12:29-31) All the rest of the Law gives practical definition to these two commandments. The two cannot be easily separated.

Yeshua said that, "All the Law and the Prophets are suspended from these two commandments." (Matt. 22:40) So only if these two great commandments were revoked could the Law be abolished.

Yeshua affirmed that he did not come to abolish the Law, but to establish it. (Mt.5:17) He came, died, and rose from the dead so that the requirements of the Law might be fulfilled in his followers. (cf. Rom.8:3-4) He came to empower people to love God and to love their neighbor. For, "The entire law is summed up in a single commandment: 'Love your neighbor as yourself.' " (Gal. 5:14)

God's Law, like the One from whom it comes, is holy, righteous, and good. (cf. Rom.7:12) That is why those who love God can say, "Oh, how I love Your law! I meditate on it all day long.... I hate double-minded men, but I love Your law.... I hate and abhor falsehood, but I love Your law. Seven times a day I praise You for Your righteous laws. Great peace have they who love Your law, and nothing can make them stumble. (Ps. 119:97,113,163-165)

Love does not stand in opposition to God's holy, righteous, good Law. It is love that enables the Law to stand. (cf. Rom.13:8-10)

Yeshua came in love to take the punishment that our sins have earned. He came to justify us, but He did not come to justify our sins. He did not come to redefine sin. When we put our faith in him, we put our faith in his righteousness, the righteousness of a life lived in perfect obedience to God's Law.

Faith does not stand in opposition to God's Law. The Law itself testifies that there is a righteousness that comes from faith. (cf. Rom.3:21) Faith is the means by which the Law is established. (cf. Rom.3:31)

THE PROBLEM WITH INTERPRETING THE SCRIPTURES BACKWARDS

Some traditional teachings of the Church are backwards, the exact opposite of what the Scriptures actually teach. It was not always that way. It happened over time.

How did it happen? The Church began to approach the Scriptures by beginning in the "New Testament," forming an understanding of its teachings, and then going backwards to approach the Scriptures which God gave first. One way or another, often through denying the plain meaning of the text or ignoring it altogether, the Bible was made to conform to the changing location and ideology of the Church.

Historically, logically, and Biblically this approach is wrong. Historically, the followers of Yeshua did not simply accept whatever new teaching they heard. They tested what they heard against what God had already revealed to Israel at Sinai and in the thousand years following.

Logically, they couldn't have tested the established revelation, which they knew to be true, by a new revelation which they did not know to be true. The Law, the Writings, and the Prophets were accepted, acknowledged, and established as God's Truth. Biblically, God had commanded, and Yeshua affirmed, that a new teaching or claim of Messiahship be tested against what God had already revealed. The new had to be measured by the Truth, not vice versa.

Interpreting the Bible backwards produces a message, a teaching, that is backwards. Beginning at the end both obscures the beginning and trivializes all of history that doesn't fit into an assumed triumphalist march. The last chapter is indeed a conclusion, but what is it that is being concluded? Beginning at the end invites, it almost insures, that one will read into the text what one thinks it should say, rather than read out of the text what it actually does say.

Equally devastating is the fact that this approach provides absolutely no basis for demonstrating the authenticity of the "New Testament" or of the Messiahship of Yeshua. It simply assumes both. That, however, is not consistent with the "New Testament" itself. Nor is it faith. It is only presumption.

How can anyone know that the "New Testament" really is what it claims to be? How can anyone know that Yeshua is the Messiah? How should anyone know?

There are many religions that have their own holy books which claim to be the authentic revelation of God, even the culmination of and the key to understanding all that came before. How can we know whether any such claim is true or false?

Is the Koran what it claims to be? Is the Book of Mormon? Is the Talmud? They all claim to be the correct interpretation of the Hebrew scriptures.

What about the many other books which make the same claim of divine inspiration and authority? Each book, each religion, claims to be true, no matter what its teaching. Judged only by itself, each is true, even as all the ways of a man are right in his own eyes.

It is pointless to discuss what is true and what is false if we do not agree on the standard by which such judgments should be made. It is pointless to discuss the implications of what God has said when we do not agree on the proper way to identify or understand what He has said.

A particular religion's proclamation of a teaching does not make the teaching true. Nor does a particular religion's rejection of some teaching make that teaching necessarily false. To those who already believe in that religion's authenticity and authority, such acceptance and rejection are indeed authoritative, but that begs the primary questions: What is the basis for the claim of authority? How can it be tested? When it is tested, is the claim substantiated?

How could anyone in the first century, or today for that matter, know whether the teachings in the gospels, in the letters, and in Revelation are true or false? Put yourself in the first century when the teaching of Yeshua and his disciples first went forth. "The religious authorities say it is true," or "The religious authorities say it is false," is not a sufficient answer.

If there is a God who has revealed Himself so that people might know Him, then each individual is responsible before God for judging whether these teachings are true or false. If you want to know and do what is pleasing to God, you need to be able to determine whether or not a teaching is from God or not. You need to be able to determine whether or not Yeshua is the Messiah. There were others then, as there are today, who claimed to be the Messiah. There are many who claim to bring a new relevation. How do you know which claim, if any, is true?

Any claim to authenticity must be based on what is already acknowledged to be true. The claim to New Covenant or Messianic authenticity must be based on what is already known to be from God. That is why we are told throughout the "New Testament" that Yeshua — who he is, what he said, what he did, etc. fulfills what was promised in the Law, the prophets, and the writings. These are referred to by the Hebrew acronym TaNaKh for *Torah, Neviim, Ketuvim* .

The New Covenant scriptures base their claim to authenticity upon Tanakh. Matthew 1 begins with a genealogy. Why? Though unimportant in all the creeds of the Church, that genealogy qualifies Yeshua to be considered as possibly being the Messiah. Without that genealogy, he could not be the Messiah.

We are told repeatedly throughout the gospels that, "This was done that it might be fulfilled..." The purpose is to demonstrate that Yeshua is the promised Messiah, because, as Revelation 19:10 says, "the testimony of Yeshua is the spirit of prophecy." It is fulfilled prophecy that testifies of who he is.

If Yeshua, or any other Messianic claimant, does not fulfill the prophetic Messianic promises, then he is not the Messiah and people should not believe in him. **To reject Tanakh — the prior, authoritative revelation of God — is to reject the Biblical basis for determining who is and who is not the Messiah.**

In John 5:45-47, Yeshua told those around Him that their failure to believe in Him was due to their failure to believe the writings of Moses. "If you believed Moses you would believe me for he wrote of me. But if you do not believe his writings how will you believe my words." **Anyone who rejects what Moses wrote will have no basis for believing, or even understanding, what Yeshua said.**

The Law of Moses leads us to Yeshua. It is our tutor for that purpose. It defines Messiah. It did for the disciples. "Philip found Nathanael and told him, 'We have found the one Moses wrote about in the

Law, and about whom the prophets also wrote —
Yeshua of Nazareth, the son of Joseph.'" (John 1:45)

The foundation of Yeshua's teaching is Tanakh.
After Yeshua had risen from the dead, He taught his
disciples so that they would understand correctly and
accurately. He taught them what they later wrote
down, lived by, and taught to succeeding generations
of disciples. "And beginning with Moses and all the
prophets, he explained to them the things concerning
himself in all the scriptures." (Luke 24:27)

What Yeshua taught his disciples had to come out
of what God had already revealed and taught Israel.
It could not contradict it in any way, or the disciples
were commanded by God to reject it. (e.g. Dt. 12:32-
13:18) It could contradict their prior understanding
of the text, but not the text itself. If the new teaching
called them to turn away from the God of Israel, they
were to reject it, even if it were confirmed with signs
and wonders. (Dt.13:1-18)

In a following incident, Yeshua told his disciples,
"These are my words which I spoke to you while I
was still with you that all things which are written
about me in the Law of Moses and the prophets and
the Psalms must be fulfilled. Then he opened their
mind to understand the scriptures." (Luke 24:44-45)
Their faith had to be based on the Scriptures.

His teaching, its source and foundation, was to
be found there. His disciples needed to know him
and his message, so he taught them from Tanakh.

**The foundation of all of Paul's teaching was also
Tanakh.** If Paul was going to be faithful to Yeshua
and what Yeshua taught, it had to be so. "For what I
received I passed on to you as of first importance:
that Messiah died for our sins according to the
Scriptures, that he was buried, that he was raised on

the third day according to the Scriptures." (1Cor. 15:3-4)

When Paul was on trial for his life, he said, "Neither in the Temple, nor in the synagogue, nor in the city did they find me carrying on a discussion with anyone or causing a riot nor can they prove to you the charges of which they now accuse me, but this I admit to you that according to the way which they call a sect, I do serve the God of our fathers believing everything that is accordance with the Law and that is written in the prophets." (Acts 24:12-14)

If it didn't agree with the Law and the prophets, Paul didn't believe it. Defending himself in the ongoing trial for his life, Paul said, "Now I am standing trial for the hope of the promise made by God to our fathers." (Acts 26:6) That was why he was on trial. Not for some completely new teaching that had just appeared, but because of the promise of God to Abraham, Isaac, and Jacob.

"And so having obtained help from God, I stand to this day testifying both to small and great stating nothing but what the prophets and Moses said was going to take place." (Acts 26:22) Paul maintained that his message came from what is in Moses and the prophets. That was the foundation of his teaching. As Paul wrote to the believers in Corinth, "Do I say this merely from a human point of view? Doesn't the Law say the same thing?" (1Cor. 9:8)

The Spirit of God gave Paul understanding that others hadn't had, but it was still an understanding of what God had already said. On trial for his life, he was not afraid to die but he was not guilty of doing what he was accused of doing. He was only guilty of believing the promises of God to Israel.

When he was under house arrest in Rome, Paul

called the Jewish community to himself to communicate exactly what his message was, what the promise of God to the Fathers of Israel and their hope was. "And when they had set a day for him, they came to him at his lodging in large numbers, and he was explaining to them by solemnly testifying to the kingdom of God and trying to persuade them concerning Yeshua from both the Law of Moses and from the prophets from morning until evening." (Acts 28:23)

Paul's message came from the Law and the prophets. He spoke from the Law and the prophets to convince people, to demonstrate that Yeshua is the prophesied Messiah. He tried to convince them in Rome, and everywhere else, that the kingdom of God that he proclaimed was what had already been written, already promised, in the acknowledged, authentic revelation of God, i.e. Tanakh. The Holy Spirit taught him, but the Holy Spirit taught him from Tanakh. Spiritually, logically, it could not be any other way.

How could a first century Jew know whether what Paul was proclaiming was true or not? How could anyone know? In Thessalonica, "As his custom was, Paul went into the synagogue, and on three Sabbath days he reasoned with them from the Scriptures, explaining and proving that the Messiah had to suffer and rise from the dead. 'This Yeshua I am proclaiming to you is the Messiah,' he said." (Acts 17:2-3) Paul based his case for the Messiahship of Yeshua upon Tanakh.

The Scriptures commend the Jews in the synagogue in Berea, where Paul went from Thessalonica. "Now these were more noble minded than those in Thessalonica for they received the word with great eagerness, examining the Scriptures daily to see if these things were so." (Acts 17:11) Paul preached to them, and they examined the Scriptures to see whether what he was saying was true or not. They are commended for checking Paul's teaching against Tanakh.

If his teaching did not agree with the Scriptures, then it was not true, and they were commanded by God to reject him and the teaching he brought. The Lord warned Israel to judge spiritual messages by looking "To the Law and to the testimony! If they do not speak according to this word, the light has not dawned on them." (Is. 8:20)

"These were more noble-minded...because they searched the Scriptures..." They searched the only Scriptures there were — the Law, the writings, and the prophets. They searched them daily to see if this new teaching was true or not. God commended them for that. God requires that of all Israel.

That was the only way they could tell whether or not the teaching was true. If it agreed with Tanakh, they should accept it. If it disagreed with Tanakh, God required that they reject it. The result of their testing Paul's teaching by the standard of Tanakh was that, "Many of them **therefore** believed, along with a number of prominent Greek women and men." (Acts 17:12)

The acknowledged Word of God could not be judged — accepted or rejected — by some later revelation. It was the new revelation that had to be judged. If the new revelation did not agree with what was known to be from God, then the new revelation had to be rejected.

Historically, logically, and Biblically it could not be any other way. To establish a point, Paul and all the writers of the New Covenant scriptures refer to what has already been established and accepted. They believed and taught everything that agreed with Moses and the prophets.

It is a tautology, but one which needs to be stated: Those who do not believe as Yeshua and Paul did have a faith that is different from that of Yeshua and Paul.

THE BOOK, THE LAW, OR THE COVENANT?

A major problem for the Church in approaching and understanding the Bible developed in the second century. It was then that the term "Old Testament" was first used to refer to the first thirty-nine books of the Bible, and the term "New Testament" was first used to refer to the last 27 books of the Bible. Even though almost everyone today has come to believe that is what the terms mean, it is not what they mean in the Bible.

These Biblical terms are more accurately translated into English as "Old Covenant" and "New Covenant." When the scriptures refer to the Old Covenant, the first Covenant, or the former Covenant, they are not referring to the first 39 books of the Bible. Nor are they referring to the Law of Moses. They are referring to the Covenant of the Law, the particular agreement which God made with Israel at Sinai.

The Book

What do people mean when they say that the "Old Testament" has passed away? Do they mean that the first 39 books of the Bible are no longer true? or that the yet unfulfilled prophecies they contain will never be fulfilled? Or do they mean that any promises God made in Tanakh — including the promises of judgment for sin, and for the establishment of righteousness in the earth — are no longer promised?

After Yeshua rose from the dead, He appeared to the disciples and taught them all they needed to know to proclaim the gospel. He taught them from the only authoritative revelation of God, Tanakh.

He appeared to some disciples and said to them

"'O foolish men and slow of heart to believe all that the prophets have spoken. Was it not necessary for Messiah to suffer these things and to enter into his glory?' And beginning with Moses and all the prophets, He explained to them the things concerning himself in all the scriptures." (Lk.24:25-27)

The Scriptures prophetically describe the life, death, and resurrection of the Messiah. The fulfillment of those prophecies demonstrates that Yeshua is the Messiah. The faith of the disciples had to be based on Moses, the prophets, and all the Scriptures, i.e. Tanakh. They needed to understand Tanakh to be able to proclaim the gospel, to present Yeshua as the fulfillment of the Messianic prophecies.

On another occasion he said to them, "These are my words which I spoke to you while I was still with you that all things that are written about me in the Law of Moses and the prophets, and the psalms must be fulfilled." Then he opened their minds to understand the Scriptures." (Lk.24:44,45)

To know Yeshua, they had to know the Scriptures. The Law, the Writings, and the Prophets were the only written Word. Yeshua is the living Word. "The Word became flesh and dwelt among us...." (Jn.1:14)

In the gospels, none of the disciples ever quoted a single word of scripture. After Yeshua taught them, that changed. Peter quoted scripture after scripture in his first public speech on Shavuos. The quotations placed the pouring out of God's Spirit as the fulfillment of what God had promised and was then fulfilling.

Peter always called the people to pay attention to what God had said in Tanakh: "And we have the more certain prophetic word, and you will do well to pay attention to it, as to a light shining in a dark place, until the day dawns and the morning star rises in your hearts." (2Pet. 1:19)

In all their writings, John and Paul also presented Tanakh as the foundation of all they taught and proclaimed. They quote from it to establish a point. Even in Revelation, the last book of the Bible, John quotes from the Law, the writings, and the prophets, speaking of their future fulfillment.

After Adam's sin, God pronounced judgment on Adam, Eve, the serpent, and the earth. That judgment still stands, and all of Adam's descendants are still afflicted by the curse God then pronounced.

After the flood, God made a covenant with Noah promising a rainbow as a sign that He would never again destroy the earth with a flood. That promise has not passed away. He said it would endure as long as the earth, its seasons, and day and night did.

God promised Abraham that he would be heir of all the earth. That promise has not passed away. All believers, even those who are Gentiles, must be children of Abraham to share in what God promised to Abraham. This is very important, ongoing Truth. (Rom. 4; Gal. 3)

Paul wrote about all the things that happened to Israel in the wilderness that, "These things happened to them as an example and they were written for our instruction upon whom the ends of the ages have come." (I Cor 10:11) The Scriptures are still God's Truth, and they still instruct us as to how we should live — even until the end of this age.

God doesn't change. Humanity doesn't change either. The same issues that arose in the time of Genesis, Exodus, Leviticus, Numbers, and Deuteronomy still arise today.

Paul instructed Timothy to raise up faithful men

and teach them what Paul had taught him. "Evil men and imposters will proceed from bad to worse deceiving and being deceived. You, however, continue in the things you have learned and become convinced of knowing from whom you have learned them and that from childhood you have known the sacred writings which are able to give you the wisdom that leads to salvation through faith which is in Yeshua, the Messiah. All scripture is breathed by God and profitable for teaching, for reproof, for correction, for training in righteousness, that the man of God may be adequate, equipped for every good work." (2Tim.3:14-17)

The Scriptures which Timothy had known from childhood were not the gospels and letters. They hadn't been written yet. Timothy had known Tanakh. These are the Scriptures which Paul says are able to give the wisdom that leads to salvation through faith in Messiah. It is these Scriptures, given by God's Spirit, which Paul considered necessary to train people in the knowledge and service of God.

Neither Paul nor Peter nor Yeshua nor any writer from Matthew to Revelation taught that the first 39 books of the Bible had passed away. They all proclaimed them to be the foundation of a life pleasing to God.

The Lord says in Isaiah 40:8 "the grass withers, the flower fades, but the Word of the Lord endures forever." If the 80% of the Word of the Lord that is Tanakh has passed away already, what hope is there for the remaining 20%?

The Law of Moses

Sometimes some Christians think that "Old Testament" means the Law of Moses, and that the

Law of Moses has passed away. In commenting on Paul's letter to the Galatians, Martin Luther taught that, "Christ has abolished all the laws of Moses that ever were."[1]

What a terrible thing that would be if it were true. There would be no laws against murder, theft, idolatry, adultery, bearing false witness, dishonoring one's parents, and on and on. Imagine the evil let loose in a world where God neither prohibits anything nor commands anything.

Fortunately, Messiah did the opposite of what Luther claimed. The Law is eternal. It cannot be abolished or destroyed. It is spiritual, holy, righteous, and good. God gave it and God breathed it. Like all the Word of God, it doesn't pass away. Luther and others have grossly misrepresented the teachings of Paul.

The historical record is actually very clear, and indisputable. All the apostles, including Paul, lived in accordance with the Law of Moses. All the Jewish believers did.

Irenaeus was a disciple of Polycarp, the disciple of the apostle John. About 180 A.D., he wrote a book "Against Heresies", to safeguard the faith delivered by the apostles. He recorded some simple historical facts.

"And the Apostles who were with Jacob [i.e., "James" in English translations] allowed the Gentiles to act freely, yielding us up to the Spirit of God. But they themselves, while knowing the same God, continued in the ancient observances...Thus did the Apostles, whom the Lord made witnesses of every action and of every doctrine...scrupulously act according to the dispensation of the Mosaic law..."[2]

Other historical sources indicate the same. There is no historical evidence to the contrary.

The Law is the means by which we know what sin is. As Paul writes in Romans 7:7: "What shall we say then is the Law sin? May it never be. On the contrary, I would not have come to know sin except through the Law for I would not have known coveting if the Law had not said you shall not covet." The Law defines and prohibits sin. "And where there is no law there is no transgression." (Rom. 4:15)

Paul recognized that, "until the Law sin was in the world, but sin is not imputed when there is no law." (Rom. 5:13) If there is no law forbidding something, then it is not forbidden. If there were no law at all, then nothing would be forbidden. Nothing would be sin. Nothing would be wrong, and there would be no need or meaning for admonitions like, "Do not continue to present the members of your body to serve sin and lawlessness; but give yourselves to God as people resurrected from the dead to serve God in righteousness." (Rom.6:13)

Sin is lawlessness. It is breaking God's Law. (cf. 1Jn. 3:4, Rom 2:12b) It is doing what is wrong. The Law shows us what is right. It shows us what loving our neighbor is. It shows us what loving God is.

If there were no law, then there would be no sin, there would be no sinners, and there would be no judgment, because there would be nothing to judge people for, and nothing to judge people by. There would then be no need for grace or salvation or a savior, because there would be nothing from which to be saved. On the contrary, however, the wrath of God will be poured out on the disobedient, those who have rejected His commandments.

If there were no law or commandment, then there

would be no right or wrong. Paul understood the Law to be our tutor. It teaches us what righteousness and love are. It teaches us of God's justice and judgment. It leads us to Messiah. As Moses said to Israel, "And what other nation is so great as to have such righteous decrees and laws as this body of laws I am setting before you today?" (Dt.4:8)

The way Paul quotes from the Law indicates his view of it. For example, "Children, obey your parents in the Lord, for this is right. 'Honor your father and mother' – which is the first commandment with a promise – 'that it may go well with you and that you may enjoy long life on the earth.' " (Eph.6:1-3)

The Law says it. That settles it. The promise is still operational.

Yeshua taught that everyone would be judged for their sins. So did Paul. So did Peter. So did John. They never taught that God's Law had passed away.

The Covenant of the Law

" 'Behold days are coming,' declares the Lord, 'when I will make a new covenant with the house of Israel and with the house of Judah, not like the covenant which I made with their fathers in the day I took them by the hand to bring them out of the land of Egypt, My covenant which they broke although I was a husband to them,' declares the Lord." (Jer. 31:31-34)

God promised to make a new covenant with Israel — the same Israel which He brought out of Egypt, the same Israel which later broke the Covenant of the Law. God had promised judgment, destruction, and ultimately exile for breaking the covenant He established at Sinai. That was being fulfilled in the time of Jeremiah. The northern kingdom of Israel was already in exile, and not much was left of the southern kingdom of Judah.

In the midst of this judgment for breaking the covenant made at Sinai, God declared His faithfulness to Israel. Though our fathers broke the covenant which He made with us at Sinai, God promised to make a new covenant. His choice and His purpose remained the same.

The "Old Covenant" is the agreement that God made with Israel at Sinai. It contains a specific revelation of God's Law with specific details to demonstrate to and through Israel the righteousness of God, the necessity of faith and obedience, and the nature of Messiah. It was God's gracious gift.

God had chosen Israel long before Sinai when He chose Abraham, Isaac, and Jacob. Being chosen preceded redemption. It was because God had chosen Israel that He redeemed Israel. It was because God had redeemed Israel that He gave Israel the Law.

The Law itself was not given as a means of salvation or redemption. Redemption from Egypt preceded the giving of the Law. The Law taught the chosen, redeemed people how to live before God.

If your father were king and you were a young child destined to rule one day, he would get a tutor to train you and teach you what you would need to know to rule the kingdom when your time came. He would give the tutor authority to teach, discipline, and punish you.

When your time came, would you immediately shoot your tutor, reject everything he had ever taught you, and then have the audacity to proclaim your actions to be in accordance with the wishes, desires, and intentions of your father the king? The tutor is not the king. He is given by the king to train those who will one day rule. They must be trained so that they can properly make decisions and act in the liberty, freedom, responsibility, and position they will one day have.

The tutor is there so that you might take his lessons to heart, so that they might become a natural part of your thought processes. You are to rule according to what you have learned, even though the tutor no longer has authority to control or punish you. You will not need to be controlled from the outside, because you will have accepted what you have been taught. You will be controlled from within your own heart. It will be your second nature.

The Covenant of the Law was given out of God's love, mercy, and grace, but it promised judgment and death to those who broke it. The New Covenant is not God's means of destroying His Law. It is His means of establishing it.

"I will write my Law within you. I will write it on your hearts and put it in your minds." God writes His Law on our minds and on our hearts so that we may remember and do all His commandments and be holy to Him. His Law is still His standard of holiness and righteousness. He puts His spirit within us to enable us to walk in obedience.

That's why Yeshua said, "Don't even think that I came to destroy the Law. I didn't come to destroy it, but to bring it to fullness/to fulfill it/to establish it." All Israel had proclaimed many years before: "Cursed is he who does not confirm/fulfill/raise up the words of this law by doing them." (Dt.27:26)

As King of the Jews, Yeshua lived according to the holy law which God had given to Israel. That Law was breathed by God, given by His Spirit. Yeshua lived in harmony with the Law, because he lived in harmony with the Spirit.

That's why Paul wrote, "Do we then abolish the Law by faith? God forbid. We establish it." (Rom.3:31) That's the whole purpose, that the righteousness of God might be established in us.

As Paul said of the New Covenant, Yeshua atoned for our sins and we received the Holy Spirit "so that the righteous requirements of the Law might be fully met in us, who do not live according to the sinful nature but according to the Spirit." (Rom. 8:4)

I am guilty and condemned by the Law. As my kinsman-redeemer, Yeshua paid the penalty of death for my sins. If I accept his payment through identification with him, the judgment of the Law against me has been carried out and satisfied. I cannot be put into double jeopardy and condemned for the same crime after the penalty has already been paid.

God has always commended and desired righteousness, according to His revealed standard. "Blessed is the man who does not walk in the counsel of the wicked or stand in the way of sinners or sit in the seat of mockers. But his delight is in the Law of the LORD, and on His Law he meditates day and night. He is like a tree planted by streams of water, which yields its fruit in season and whose leaf does not wither. Whatever he does prospers." (Ps.1:1-3)

FOOTNOTES

1. Commentary on Galatians, Martin Luther, Translated by Erasmus Middletown, Kregel Publications, Grand Rapids, MI, 1976, P.223

2. Ante-Nicene Christian Library, Vol.5/1, trans. by A. Roberts and J. Donaldson, T & T Clark, Edinburgh, 1867, Pp.313-314

PAUL THE JEW

Many people today who do not believe that Yeshua is the Messiah are still willing to recognize him as a faithful Jew. They see Paul, however, as a non-Jew, an apostate who created a new religion. Traditional Christian theology has presented Paul that way for many centuries, but it was not the way he saw himself.

Paul was a faithful Jew, and he always thought of himself that way. As a faithful Jew, he was called to be the apostle to the Gentiles Because people have not understood the context of what Paul was saying and doing among the Gentiles, they have confused or distorted his identity. We can see his identity clearly as we follow him through the book of Acts.

Saul of Tarsus, who was also known as Paul, went to Damascus to put an end to what he considered hesesy — faith in Yeshua as the Messiah. He had sought out and brought with him letters from the high priest authorizing him to go to the synagogues in Damascus, weed out the Jews who believed in Yeshua, arrest them, and then bring them back in chains to Jerusalem to be punished for their faith. Saul believed their faith was heresy, and, being zealous for God, wanted to put an end to it.

On the way, he was supernaturally knocked to the ground and blinded, and he heard a voice from heaven speaking to him. As a Pharisee, Paul was very familiar with other occasions when God had spoken from heaven. In the Pharisaic tradition at that time, the voice from heaven, called *Bat Kol*, was always authoritative and to be obeyed. [About 50 years later, the dominant group within the Pharisees, Beit Shammai, was overthrown and another group, Beit

Hillel, took control. They rejected the teachings of Beit Shammai, and ruled that the voice of God from heaven was not authoritative.]

Saul knew who was speaking to him, but not why, so he asked the Lord to characterize Himself, saying, "Who are you Lord?" The Lord answered, "I am Yeshua whom you are persecuting. Rise and enter the city and it shall be told you what you must do." (Acts.9:5)

Saul was led into the city, where he began to fast and pray. During that time the Lord spoke to a Jewish man named Ananias and told him to go to Saul of Tarsus, and pray for him. Ananias was "a devout man according to the standard of the Law." (Acts 22:12) He was the one the Lord chose to represent Himself to Saul.

Ananias was not eager to go because he knew why Saul had come. The Lord told Ananias, "Go for he is a chosen vessel of Mine to bear My name before the Gentiles and kings and the sons of Israel." (Acts 9:15) Saul of Tarsus, Paul the Jew, was called to be the apostle to the Gentiles, a light to the nations.

Years later, Paul was in Antioch fasting and praying, and the Lord told him to begin to travel to fulfill that calling. So he and Barnabas went to Salamis in Cyprus, went into the synagogue, and proclaimed that Yeshua is the Messiah. The synagogue was the only place where the message could be understood. It was the only place where the word of God was being studied, where people were seeking to know the Lord, and where there was an expectation of Messiah.

They travelled on to Antioch in Pisidia, went into the synagogue, and delivered the message of Yeshua as the Messiah. Some believed and some didn't.

That's what happened everywhere. In Antioch, however, the Gentiles of the city asked if they could also hear this message. "The next Sabbath nearly the whole city assembled to hear the word of God. When the Jews saw the crowds they were filled with jealously and began contradicting the things spoken by Paul and were blaspheming." (Acts13:44)

Some Jews who hadn't believed were jealous of the interest that the whole city was showing in Paul's message. They knew that the Lord had created Israel to bring the Gentiles out of darkness and back to Himself. They knew that they had not done that. They saw that Paul was doing that. They were jealous and began speaking against what Paul was saying.

Paul and Barnabus responded to them, "It was necessary that the word of God should be spoken to you first. Since you repudiate it and judge yourselves unworthy of eternal life, behold we are turning to the Gentiles, because this is what the Lord has commanded us: 'I have placed you as a light for the Gentiles that you should bring salvation to the end of the earth.' " (Acts 13:46-47) That is what the Lord had told all Israel through Isaiah the prophet.

Paul saw himself as fulfilling this responsibility. Every other Jew had to make his or her own choice. Paul saw himself as a Jew being faithful to what God commanded all Israel to do — to be a light to the Gentiles.

From Antioch, Paul went to Iconium, went into the synagogue to deliver God's message. A great multitude believed, and some didn't. (Acts 14:1)

The next chapter of Acts, 15, describes the Council in Jerusalem wrestling with the question of the relationship to the Law of Moses of Gentiles who believed. "Then some of the believers who belonged to the party of the Pharisees stood up and said, 'The Gentiles must be circumcised and required to obey the law of Moses.' The apostles and elders met to consider this question." (Acts 15:5-6)

All the Jewish believers, and proselytes who had become believers, faithfully observed circumcision, the sign of God's covenant with Abraham, and lived according to the law of Moses. They understood the Scriptures to say that the new Gentile disciples also had to do the same. They had to become Jewish and enter into God's covenant with Israel made at Sinai in order to enter into Israel's New Covenant.

If the apostles, elders and other Jewish believers had rejected circumcision and were not themselves obeying the law of Moses, there would have been nothing to discuss. There would have been no question to consider concerning the Gentiles. However, the apostles themselves would then have been guilty under Roman law for starting a new, unauthorized religion.

Peter explained what happened when God sent him to the Gentiles. Paul and Barnabas also spoke, relating what God was doing among the Gentiles to what He had promised through the prophets. The Council concluded that the Gentiles do not have to become Jewish, they do not need to be circumcised and keep the Law of Moses, in order to follow Messiah.

Of course the God of Israel is the God of the Jews, but is He only the God of the Jews? or is He the God of all? If He is only the God of the Jews, then the Gentiles must become Jews in order to serve Him. The God of Israel, however, is the Creator, Redeemer, and Judge of all. There is only one true God, whom both Jew and Gentile must obey, but He deals with them differently, according to what He has created each to be.

That was the conclusion of the Council. To encourage the Gentiles to do that properly, the Council reminded them of four universal laws which they needed to obey. There are other universal laws, like the prohibition of murder and theft, which the Council did not consider necessary to mention, because all Gentiles were well aware that God expected these things of them.

Sometime after the Council Paul continued travelling (Acts 16) and came to Derbe, where there was a young disciple named Timothy, whose mother was Jewish and whose father was Greek. Timothy had a reputation as a solid young believer. Paul wanted Timothy to travel and minister with him, but Timothy was uncircumcised. To bring Timothy into obedience to God's commandment to Abraham, Paul circumcised him. As they came to congregations of believers, they delivered the decrees which the Jerusalem Council had affirmed as binding for all Gentiles. That included the conclusion that Gentile believers did not need to be circumcised.

They came to Phillippi where apparently there were not enough Jews to have a synagogue. Those there met by the river on Shabbat at a *proseuche*, a place of prayer. Paul told those who were gathered there about Yeshua the Messiah.

Then he "came to Thessalonica, where there was a synagogue of the Jews and according to Paul's custom he went to them and for three Sabbaths reasoned with them from the Scriptures." Paul always sought to persuade his fellow Jews that Yeshua is the Messiah. If he had been unable to demonstrate that from the Law, the writings, and the prophets, then no one would have, or should have, believed him. So he gave the Biblical evidence. Some believed, some didn't.

From there he went to Berea, into the synagogue. The Jews there "were more noble minded than those in Thessalonica, for they received the word with great eagerness examining the Scriptures daily to see whether these things were so. Many of them therefore believed..." (Acts 17:11-12) Because these Jews carefully compared Paul's message with the Scriptures daily, many of them believed. Even as Yeshua had said, "If you believed Moses, you would believe me because he wrote of me." (Jn.5:46)

From there Paul went to Athens where he saw a city filled with idols, "and his spirit was provoked within him. Therefore, he was reasoning in the synagogue with the Jews and the god-fearing [Gentiles], and in the marketplace everyday with those who happened to be present." (Acts 17:17)

Paul's reaction to the idolatry of Athens was to go into the synagogue. His reasoning was that God has commanded the Jewish people to be a light to the Gentiles, to bring His salvation to the ends of the earth.

The Gentiles in Athens were in a darkness of their own choosing, but no one was bringing the light to them. So Paul reasoned with the Jews of Athens that they might follow Messiah the King and bring the salvation of God to the ends of the earth, to all the Gentiles.

Paul then went to Corinth "and he was reasoning in the synagogue every Sabbath and trying to persuade Jews and Greeks." (Acts 18:4) As in every other place, some believed and some didn't. Some rejected the message and spoke fervently against it.

Paul spoke as fervently in response: "Your blood be on your own heads! I am clear of my responsibility. From now on I will go to the Gentiles." (Acts 18:6)

Paul saw his responsibility as the same that God had required of Ezekiel. God told Ezekiel that it was necessary for him to warn the people to turn from their sins, otherwise their blood would be on his head. If Ezekiel were to warn them, whether or not they believed him, he would have delivered his own soul. (Ezek. 3 & 33)

Paul spoke in prophetic terms to say, "I have warned you. Your blood is on your own head now. I have delivered my own soul." He said much the same later to the leaders of the believers in Ephesus: "I declare to you today that I am innocent of the blood of all men, for I have not hesitated to proclaim to you the whole will of God." (Acts 20:26-27)

When Paul said in Corinth, "from now on I will go to the Gentiles," he did not mean that he would not go to the Jews any more, but only that he would **also** go to the Gentiles. Paul moved next door to the synagogue, and subsequently the leader of the synagogue and his entire family came to faith in Yeshua. (Acts 18:8)

The new leader of the synagogue, Sosthenes, was very upset, and brought Paul before the judge to try to get him imprisoned and punished. The judge was not interested, and Sosthenes himself was beaten. Sosthenes later became a believer and travelled with Paul to spread the gospel. (cf. 1 Co.1:1)

In Cenchrea, Paul had his hair shaved to keep a vow according to the Law of Moses. (Acts18:18) Paul then went to Ephesus into the synagogue to reason with his fellow Jews. (Acts18:19) They wanted him to stay longer, but he needed to leave, promising to return when he could. When Paul returned to Ephesus, he went again into the synagogue to reason with and persuade those there about the kingdom of God. (Acts 19:8)

Paul observed Passover in the Diaspora, but cut short his ministry so that he could be in Jerusalem for Shavuos, i.e. Pentecost. (Acts 20:6,16) He fasted in observance of Yom Kippur. (Acts 27:9) As a Jew, Paul observed the feasts of the Lord.

When he arrived in Jerusalem, he went to tell Jacob and the other Messianic Jewish leaders what great things God had done among the goyim, the Gentiles. When they heard it, they glorified God for opening blinded Gentile eyes.

There was, however, one very important matter that needed to be settled once and for all. The leaders said to Paul: "You see brother how many myriads there are among the Jews of those who have believed and they are all zealous for the Law. And they have been told about you that you are teaching all the Jews who are among the Gentiles to forsake Moses, telling them not to circumcise their children nor to walk according to the customs.

"What then is to be done? They will certainly hear that you have come, so do this that we tell you. We have four men who are under a vow, take them, purify yourself according to the Law along with them, pay their expenses at the end of their purification in order that they may shave their heads and all may know that there is nothing to the things which they have been told about you, but that you yourself also walk orderly keeping the Law." (Acts 21:19-26)

The tens of thousands of Jewish believers in Jerusalem, including the apostles, were all zealous for the Law of Moses. They had heard rumors about Paul that he taught Jews to reject the Law of Moses, to stop circumcising their children, and to forsake the Jewish customs. The leaders knew that these rumors were false. It was necessary for Paul to clearly and unequivocally show to everyone that the rumors were false.

There were four Jewish followers of Yeshua who had taken a vow, even as Paul himself had earlier done. Paul purified himself according to the Law of Moses, and paid for the Temple sacrifices at the conclusion of the time of purification to demonstrate once and for all that, as a Jew, he walked according to the Law of Moses and the Jewish customs.

[In the Greek text, there is one word, *ethesin*, that signifies the customs of the people as a whole. There is another word, *paradosin*, that signifies the traditions of the Pharisees.]

Traditional theology teaches that the rumors were actually true, i.e. Paul did not really keep the Law of Moses and the Jewish customs. If that were true, it would mean that Paul intentionally deceived the other apostles and everyone else by hypocritically doing what he had openly condemned elsewhere.

Those who teach that he did this suppose that when Paul left Jerusalem he continued to teach Jews to reject the Law of Moses, to reject God's covenant of circumcision with Abraham, and to reject the customs of the Jewish people. In other words, they teach that Paul was a fraud.

The traditional teaching accuses Paul of serious "blunders" or "compromise." If the traditional teaching is correct, the accusations against Paul should be much stronger. He would have been guilty of the grossest hypocrisy and most malevolent deception. He would have been causing people to believe what would insure their damnation.

The Jewish believers in the Diaspora saw clearly how Paul lived among them, and knew what he taught to Jews and what he taught to Gentiles. If Paul had been deceiving the brethren in Jerusalem, the Diaspora believers would have had no difficulty in exposing him. Nor would the unbelievers. If Paul had acted with such duplicity, Jacob and the leaders in Jerusalem would have excommunicated him.

The congregations which the apostles led and taught were all zealous for the Law of Moses. If Paul had been teaching Jews to abandon God's covenant with Abraham by not circumcising their children, then Paul would have been an apostate, and would have been rejected as such. If he had been teaching Jews to reject the teaching of Moses, if he had been teaching Jews to forsake their customs and stop being Jews, he would have been rejected as an apostate. He would have been denying Yeshua the Messiah, the King of the Jews, and his coming kingdom. Yeshua came to enable Israel to fulfill its calling, not to abandon it.

Paul claimed that, "I strive always to keep my conscience clear before God and man." (Acts 24:16) He also spoke of "my way of life in Messiah Yeshua, which agrees with what I teach everywhere in every congregation." (1Cor. 4:17) Yeshua said that seeking the approval of men rather than that of God made faith impossible. (John 5:44) Paul agreed. "Am I now trying to win the approval of men, or of God? Or am I trying to please men? If I were still trying to please men, I would not be a servant of Messiah." (Gal. 1:10) Paul's claims stand in sharp opposition to the counterclaims that he compromised, deceived, and blundered in his attempts to appease men.

Traditional theology has been unable to reconcile the life Paul lived as a Jew with the message he taught as the apostle to the Gentiles. The difference between the "two Pauls" is the same as that made by the Jerusalem Council when they declared, "**But** concerning the Gentiles..." As Jews, they would continue to be Jews. The Gentile believers, however, did not need to become Jews in order to serve the King of the Jews.

As for Paul himself, as he said to the Roman authorities (Acts 22:3) and as he also said to the Jewish people (Acts 21:39), "I am a Jew." Even more, when on trial for his life before the Sanhedrin, he said, "Brethren, I am a Pharisee, a son of Pharisees. I am on trial for the hope and resurrection of the dead." (Acts 22:6)

Paul went through a series of legal trials where those who wanted him dead accused him of breaking the Law of Moses and defiling the Temple. In defending himself before Felix the governor, Paul said, "They cannot prove to you the charges they are now making against me. However, this I admit to you that according to the Way which they call a sect I do serve the God of our fathers believing everything that is in accordance with the Law and that is written in the prophets." (Acts 24:13-14)

Paul believed everything that agreed with the Law and the prophets, and rejected whatever contradicted them. As a Jew, he had a Jewish faith. "I have the same hope in God as these men, that there will be a resurrection of both the righteous and the wicked. In view of this I also do my best to maintain always a blameless conscience before God and before men." (Acts 24:15-16) He had a Biblical hope.

Paul always identified himself with Israel and the Jewish people. "After several years I came to bring alms to my nation and to present offerings." (Acts 24:17) Purified according to the Law of Moses, he had just offered sacrifices in the Temple when he was attacked and arrested.

Two years later, before Festus, the new governor, Paul said, "I have committed no offense either against the law of the Jews or against the Temple or against Caesar." (Acts 25:8) Was Paul lying to the governor and the Roman court? His accusers would have produced witnesses and evidence to expose such a lie if they could have. They were unable to do that. They could not demonstrate that Paul had broken the Law of Moses in any way.

Standing before Festus and King Agrippa, Paul maintained that, "Now I am standing trial for the hope of the promise made by God to our fathers.... So having obtained help from God I stand to this day testifying both to small and great stating nothing but what the prophets and Moses said was going to take place." (Acts 26:6,22) He claimed that his message was identical with what Moses and the prophets had proclaimed. No one could demonstrate otherwise.

Paul appealed to Caesar to establish his innocence, and subsequently was sent to Rome. When he arrived in Rome, he was put under house arrest and could not go to the synagogue. So, "He called together those who were the leading men of the Jews and when they had come together, he began saying to them, 'Brethren, though I have done nothing against our people, or the customs of our fathers, yet I was arrested in Jerusalem and handed over to the Romans. They examined me and wanted to release me, because I was not guilty of any crime deserving death.' " (Acts 28:17-18)

Was Paul lying and deceiving, or was he telling the truth? The Jewish leaders set a date for the whole community to hear Paul. "They came to him at his lodging in large numbers and he was explaining to them by solemnly testifying about the kingdom of God and trying to persuade them concerning Yeshua from both the Law of Moses and from the prophets from morning until evening." (Acts 28:23)

If Paul had been unable to present the evidence from the Law and the prophets for what he believed, no one would have believed it. He wouldn't have believed it himself.

If anyone could have demonstrated that what Paul believed and the way he lived was not Jewish, then Paul would have been guilty of a capital crime. Rome recognized certain religions as legitimate. Anyone who adhered to another religion was guilty of "atheism", i.e. rejecting the approved gods. That was the later basis of Roman trials of Jewish and Gentile followers of Yeshua.

It was not a question of strategy. It was a question of identity. Who was Paul? Was he a faithful Jew or not?

Years later, chained in a Roman prison cell, Paul wrote his last letter to Timothy, saying, "I thank God, **whom I serve as my forefathers did**, with a clear conscience, as I constantly remember you in my prayers night and day." (2Tim. 1:3) Facing death, he could confidently pray as one who faithfully walked in the way that God had long before shown to Israel. This is Paul the Jew, who he was, how he saw himself, and the message he proclaimed.

PAUL THE APOSTLE TO THE GENTILES

Some people cannot reconcile the Jewish Paul of the book of Acts with the opponent of the Law that they believe the Paul who wrote the letters to be. That is because they do not understand the context of Paul's letters or the primary audience to whom they were addressed.

Paul was the apostle to the Gentiles. His God-given responsibility was to bring the Gentiles into a righteous relationship with the God of Israel through the New Covenant which Messiah brought. He makes this very clear throughout his letters. His primary audience is Gentile believers. Every time Paul refers to himself as an apostle, he is reminding his audience of his God-given authority to the Gentiles. He is very conscious of his particular calling.

"Through him and for his name's sake, we received grace and apostleship to call people from among all the Gentiles to the obedience that comes from faith." (Rom. 1:5)

"I do not want you to be unaware, brothers, that I planned many times to come to you (but have been prevented from doing so until now) in order that I might have a harvest among you, just as I have had among the other Gentiles." (Rom. 1:13)

"I have written you quite boldly on some points, as if to remind you of them again, because of the grace God gave me to be a minister of Messiah Yeshua to the Gentiles with the priestly duty of proclaiming the gospel of God, so that the Gentiles might become an offering acceptable to God, sanctified by the Holy Spirit. Therefore I glory in Messiah Yeshua in my service to God. I will not venture to speak of anything except what Messiah has accomplished through me in leading the Gentiles to obey God by what I have said and done." (Rom. 15:15-18)

"You know that as Gentiles, you were influenced and led astray to mute idols." (1Cor. 12:2)

"Formerly, when you did not know God, you were slaves to those who by nature are not gods." (Gal. 4:8) "they want you to be circumcised that they may boast about your flesh." (Gal. 6:13)

"Therefore, remember that formerly you, who are Gentiles in flesh and called 'uncircumcised' by those who call themselves 'the circumcision' (that done in the body by the hands of men)..." (Eph. 2:11)

"For this reason I, Paul, the prisoner of Messiah Yeshua for the sake of you Gentiles — Surely you have heard about the administration of God's grace that was given to me for you...To me, the least of all saints, this grace was given, to preach to the Gentiles the unfathomable riches of Messiah..." (Eph. 3:1-2,8)

"So I tell you this, and insist on it in the Lord, that you must no longer live as the rest of the Gentiles do, in the futility of their thinking." (Eph. 4:17)

"To whom God has chosen to make known what is the riches of the glory of this mystery among the Gentiles , which is Messiah in you, the hope of glory." (Col. 1:27)

"In him you were also circumcised, in the putting off of the flesh, not with a circumcision done by the hands of men but with the circumcision done by Messiah...When you were dead in your sins and in the uncircumcision of your flesh, God made you alive with Messiah. He forgave us all our sins." (Col. 2:11,13)

" ...They tell how you turned to God from idols to serve the living and true God." (1Ths. 1:9)

"And for this purpose I was appointed a herald

and an apostle ...and a teacher of the true faith to the Gentiles." (1Tim. 2:7)

The gospel had gone out from Jerusalem to the Gentiles, through Jewish believers like Paul. The Jewish believers in Jerusalem had given sacrificially in response to God's goodness to them. They suffered great persecution, and a famine had come.

So Paul wrote to and went to the congregations he had established among the Gentiles to ask them to give back a measure of the immeasurable gift they had received. Some, like the congregations in Philippi, Thessalonica, and Corinth, gave freely. Others did not. We have no record that the Gentiles in Rome gave anything, though Paul exhorted them to do so.

"Now, however, I am on my way to Jerusalem in the service of the saints there. For Macedonia and Achaia were pleased to make a contribution for the poor among the saints in Jerusalem. They were pleased to do it, and indeed they owe it to them. For if the Gentiles have shared in the Jews' spiritual blessings, they owe it to the Jews to share with them their material blessings." (Rom.15:25-27) Paul not only commanded Gentile Christians not to boast against the Jews (Rom.11:18), but he also insisted that they recognize their ongoing debt for entering into the Jewish relationship with God.

Earlier, Paul had used the response of the Gentile believers in Macedonia to encourage the Corinthians in Achaia. "And now, brothers, we want you to know about the grace that God has given the Macedonian churches. Out of the most severe trial, their overflowing joy and their extreme poverty welled up in rich generosity. For I testify that they gave as much as they were able, and even beyond their ability.

Entirely on their own, they urgently pleaded with us for the privilege of sharing in this service to the saints. And they did not do as we expected, but they gave themselves first to the Lord and then to us in keeping with God's will. So we urged Titus, since he had earlier made a beginning, to bring also to completion this act of grace on your part." (2Cor. 8:1-6)

Chapters 8 & 9 of 2 Corinthians are entirely devoted to encouraging the Gentile believers to give for this need. Paul wanted the Gentiles themselves to be an acceptable offering to God.

Because the Gentiles could enter into God's New Covenant with Israel without first becoming Jews, the message that Paul proclaimed to them was not exactly the same as that proclaimed to the Jews. Even though he knew that God had revealed that message to him in the Scriptures, Paul was somewhat uneasy about the difference, because he knew that "no prophecy of Scripture is a matter of one's own interpretation." (2Pet.1:20)

So Paul went to the apostles in Jerusalem. "I went in response to a revelation and set before them the gospel that I preach among the Gentiles. But I did this privately to those who seemed to be leaders, for fear that I was running or had run my race in vain." (Gal. 2:2)

Paul thought they might reject the gospel that he was preaching to the Gentiles. "But on the contrary, they saw that I had been entrusted with the gospel of the uncircumcision, just as Peter of the circumcision. For God, who was at work in the ministry of Peter as an apostle of the circumcision, was also at work in my ministry as an apostle to the Gentiles. Jacob, Peter and John, those reputed to be pillars, gave me and Barnabas the right hand of fellowship when they recognized the grace given to me. They agreed that we should go to the Gentiles, and they to the circumcised." (Gal. 2:7-9) [Notice that both Jacob's letter and Peter's first letter are specifically addressed to the Diaspora, i.e Jews living outside the land of Israel. (Ja.1:1; 1Pet.1:1; cf. Jn.7:35)]

They recognized Paul's authority to teach the Gentiles. He recognized their authority to teach the Jews. Paul's letters are quite understandable in this context. There was no conflict between how he lived as a Jew and what he taught as apostle to the Gentiles.

ARE NON-JEWS WITHOUT LAW?

Law is an authoritative prescription of values, distinguishing between permitted and prohibited behavior, between right and wrong, and between good and evil. Most law provides for the punishment of those who break it.

That is the case when it comes to God's Torah, whether we call it Teaching or Law. What He says is a manifestation of who He is. He cannot be separated from His Word.

As long as God is, there is Divine law that prescribes what is acceptable and what is not, what is good and what is not. There cannot be any existence without the law of God. He does not create moral neutral or "Duty Free" zones which are unrelated to who He is. Wherever He is, there is a distinction between what is acceptable and what is not, what is good and what is evil.

Was it wrong for Adam and Eve to eat of the tree of the knowledge of good and evil? If it was wrong, did they know it was wrong?

God had commanded them, "you must not eat from the tree of the knowledge of good and evil, for when you eat of it you will surely die." (Gen. 2:17) But why should they have obeyed God, and how were they to know they should? God, their Creator, built into their very being the knowledge of Himself and the necessity of obeying Him.

They knew that they had done something wrong. Disobeying the commandment of God, transgressing the law of God, they sinned. (cf. Rom.5:14-19)

They hid from God, fearing the consequences of what they had done. In response to their sin, God brought judgment on them, on all their descendants, and upon the earth itself.

Was it wrong for Cain to kill Abel? Did he know it was wrong? Did he sin in killing Abel? God acted as though Cain knew it was wrong to murder. He pronounced a curse and judgment on Cain. "Now you are under a curse and driven from the ground, which opened its mouth to receive your brother's blood from your hand. When you work the ground, it will no longer yield its crops for you. You will be a restless wanderer on the earth." (Gen. 4:11-12)

Cain and Abel both bore the image and likeness of God. That was sufficient prohibition of murder. Cain knew that.

Was it wrong for the people of Noah's generation to fill the earth with violence? Was it sin? God brought judgment on them. "The LORD saw how great man's wickedness on the earth had become, and that every inclination of the thoughts of his heart was only evil all the time....So the LORD said, 'I will wipe mankind, whom I have created, from the face of the earth — men and animals, and creatures that move along the ground, and birds of the air —for I am grieved that I have made them.' " (Gen.6:5,7)

That generation turned its thoughts and hearts away from God. They sought to destroy His image and likeness within themselves. They violated their own created nature.

When Abraham said that Sara was his sister, King Abimelech took Sara into his harem. God appeared to Abimelech in the night and said, "you're a dead man because you've taken another man's wife." (Gen.20:3) The commandment "Thou shalt not commit adultery" had not yet been given at Sinai, and would not be given there for another 400 years. King Abimelech was not Jewish anyway. He lived without the Ten Commandments engraved in stone.

Why did God say Abimelech was close to being put to death for adultery? God would not have commanded judgment for him unless Abimelech had known it was wrong to commit adultery.

Abimelech's response was, "Did he not say to me, 'She is my sister,' and didn't she also say, 'He is my brother'? I have done this with a clear conscience and clean hands." (Gen. 20:5 cf.Gen.26:10) Abimelech knew that adultery was wrong. How did he know without having been given the law at Sinai?

He knew because from the very beginning God had created Adam and Eve so that they could become one flesh. To commit adultery would be to violate that oneness which God had created.

Hundreds of years before the Law of Moses was given, God affirmed His promises to Abraham, "because Abraham obeyed My voice, and kept My charge, My commandments, My decrees, and My laws (torati)." (Gen.26:5) God's law did not begin at Sinai.

God decreed the destruction of the nations in the land of Canaan because of their idolatry and immorality. He warned Israel not to commit the same sins.

"Do not defile yourselves in any of these ways, because this is how the nations that I am going to drive out before you became defiled. Even the land was defiled; so I punished it for its sin, and the land vomited out its inhabitants. But you must keep My decrees and My laws. The native-born and the aliens living among you must not do any of these detestable things, for all these things were done by the people who lived in the land before you, and the land became defiled. And if you defile the land, it will vomit you out as it vomited out the nations that were before you." (Lev. 18:24-28, cf Lev. 20:22-23)

It is only through law that sin is identified for us, because it is law that commands what is and what is not to be done. As Paul writes, "Indeed I would not have known what sin was except through the law." (Rom. 7:7) As John reminds us, "Everyone who sins breaks the law; in fact, sin is lawlessness." (1John 3:4)

Law defines sin. Sin is breaking God's law. So if there is no law, then there is no sin and there are no sinners. There would be no cause for judgment, since there would be nothing to offend against or to be judged by. No one could do anything wrong because nothing would be defined as wrong. There would be nothing from which to be saved, and no need for God's grace.

The Bible, however, clearly teaches that God is going to bring every person into judgment. Every thought, word, and deed will be judged according to God's holy, eternal law. Those who break His law will be judged accordingly. There are laws of God that apply to everyone, and everyone can sin.

For some, the revelation of that law is what is written in every person's conscience. To them God proclaimed His law in the core of their being alone, rather than in written words. For others God's revelation includes what was written on tablets of stone.

God has given to everyone a measure of understanding of right and wrong. To say "right" and "wrong" is to indicate a standard of God, a standard for judgment, a law and commandment of God.

Adam and Eve sinned in disobeying God. Cain sinned in murdering Abel. The generation of Noah was destroyed for their sins. Abimelech would have sinned had he committed adultery with Sara. Abraham was faithful to obey the laws of God. The nations living in Canaan were destroyed because of their sins against God.

How much detail is there to the law of God which He has put in the heart of every human being? Moral and political philosophers through the ages have tried to delineate God's "natural law," i.e. the law which He implanted in the very nature of His Creation. Their conclusions have varied.

To begin to come to an understanding yourself, consider the individual laws of God's covenant with Israel which were singled out as specifically bringing a curse on those who broke them. All the people were to verbally acknowledge God's righteousness in cursing "the man," i.e. anyone, who broke these laws.

" 'Cursed is the man who carves an image or casts an idol —a thing detestable to the LORD, the work of the craftsman's hands —and sets it up in secret.' Then all the people shall say, 'Amen!'

" 'Cursed is the man who dishonors his father or his mother.' Then all the people shall say, 'Amen!"

" 'Cursed is the man who moves his neighbor's boundary stone.' Then all the people shall say, 'Amen!'

" 'Cursed is the man who leads the blind astray on the road.' Then all the people shall say, 'Amen!'

" 'Cursed is the man who withholds justice from the alien, the fatherless or the widow.' Then all the people shall say, 'Amen!'

" 'Cursed is the man who sleeps with his father's wife, for he dishonors his father's bed.' Then all the people shall say, 'Amen!'

" 'Cursed is the man who has sexual relations with any animal.' Then all the people shall say, 'Amen!'

" 'Cursed is the man who sleeps with his sister, the daughter of his father or the daughter of his mother.' Then all the people shall say, 'Amen!'

" 'Cursed is the man who sleeps with his mother-in-law.' Then all the people shall say, 'Amen!'

" 'Cursed is the man who kills his neighbor secretly.' Then all the people shall say, 'Amen!'

" 'Cursed is the man who accepts a bribe to kill an innocent person.' Then all the people shall say, 'Amen!' " (Deut. 27:15-25)

Were any of these laws not applicable to all people? God's law did not begin at Mt. Sinai. Nor is it for Jews only. If it were, there would be no basis for God to judge the Gentiles.

"Indeed, when Gentiles, who do not have the law, do by nature things required by the law, they are a law for themselves, even though they do not have the law, since they show that the requirements of the law are written on their hearts, their consciences also bearing witness, and their thoughts now accusing, now even defending them." (Rom. 2:14-15)

People are judged for doing what they know is wrong. From the beginning, God put within each person some light. We read in Romans 1 that the wrath of God is revealed from heaven against all ungodliness and unrighteousness of every person who suppresses the truth in unrighteousness. People know the truth, but they suppress it.

"Since the creation of the world his invisible attributes, his eternal power, His divine nature have been clearly seen, being understood through what has been. So they are without excuse, for even though they knew God they did not honor him as God or give thanks, but they became futile in their speculations and their foolish heart was darkened.

Professing to be wise, they became fools and exchanged the glory of the incorruptible God for an image in the form of corruptible man and of birds and of four-footed animals and crawling creatures." (vv.20-23)

These people committed idolatry and God holds them accountable for that. They were not Jewish. They did not enter into God's covenant of the law made with Israel at Sinai, but they still had the law of God in their hearts.

"They exchanged the truth of God for a lie and worshipped and served the creature rather than the Creator....And just as they did not see fit to acknowledge God any longer, God gave them over to a depraved mind....And although they know the ordinance of God that those who practice such things are worthy of death, they not only do the same but also give hearty approval to those who practice them." (vv.25, 28, 32)

They are responsible, as all people are, for their actions against God's righteousness. Long before the covenant of the law was given, God revealed these things and called men to account for them. Non-Jews are not under the law given at Sinai, but God already placed much of that law in their consciences.

The Law of Moses, contained in the covenant made at Sinai, is a specific revelation of God's righteousness in relationship to His people Israel. It was given so that He might reveal Himself in very specific ways through it. The law is our tutor to teach us faith and righteousness, and to lead us to Messiah. It was also given to set Israel apart from the Gentiles.

In the Talmud, the Rabbis discuss the universal nature of much of the law that God included in His covenant with Israel. (cf. Shab.88b, Zeb.116a) They often spoke of the laws that are binding on all the descendants of Noah.

After the flood, God said to Noah, "Everything that lives and moves will be food for you. Just as I gave you the green plants, I now give you everything, but you must not eat meat with its life, which is its blood, still in it." (Gen.9:3-4) This was and still is binding on every descendant of Noah, whether he or she believes it or not.

God will call every person to account according to the commandments He has given to each. God has given light to everyone. Everyone is without excuse.

The first-century Jerusalem Council of Jewish believers issued four specific decrees for all the Gentile followers of Yeshua to obey. "You are to abstain from food sacrificed to idols, from blood, from the meat of strangled animals and from sexual immorality. You will do well to avoid these things. (Acts 15:29)

These were all laws which God already required all Gentiles to obey. The Council was merely restating them because some of the Gentile believers were ignorant of, or hardened to, the Biblical teachings.

Idolatry, which includes sacrificing food to idols, had always been forbidden and condemned. All the descendants of Noah were already commanded not to eat the blood of any animal. The meat of a strangled animal would have its blood still in it. And God had expressly forbidden sexual immorality. That was one of the reasons why He destroyed the tribes of Canaan.

The Bible is very clear in teaching that Gentiles who break God's law are gulty of sinning against God. In the wilderness, God spoke of the immoral practices of the Canaanite tribes, and warned Israel, "Do not defile yourselves in any of these ways, because this is how the nations that I am going to drive out before you became defiled. Even the land was defiled; so I punished it for its sin, and the land vomited out its inhabitants." (Lev. 18:24-25)

Daniel advised Nebuchadnezzar, "Therefore, O king, be pleased to accept my advice: Renounce your sins by doing what is right, and your wickedness by being kind to the oppressed. It may be that then your prosperity will continue." (Dan. 4:27)

The king of Nineveh repented at the preaching of Jonah, and urged the people, " 'Let man and beast be covered with sackcloth. Let everyone call urgently on God. Let them give up their evil ways and their violence. Who knows? God may yet relent and with compassion turn from His fierce anger so that we will not perish.'

"When God saw what they did and how they turned from their evil ways, He had compassion and did not bring upon them the destruction He had threatened." (Jonah 3:8-10) They knew the evil of their ways, and they chose to repent.

God sent Peter to preach to Cornelius, a Roman centurion, and his family. The other Jewish believers rebuked Peter for eating with these Gentiles. Peter explained how Cornelius and his family feared God, and had received the Holy Spirit. "When they heard this, they had no further objections and praised God, saying, 'So then, God has granted even the Gentiles repentance unto life.' " (Acts 11:18)

Gentiles can repent of their sins, turning away from their lawless deeds, and find atonement through the death of Messiah, the King of the Jews. This is, in fact, the message that Israel, as a light to the goyim, is to bring to all the earth.

This is the message that Paul, the apostle to the

Gentiles, proclaimed throughout his ministry. Even as Paul was on trial, he steadfastly continued to proclaim this message. "As Paul discoursed on righteousness, self-control and the judgment to come, Felix was afraid and said, 'That's enough for now! You may leave. When I find it convenient, I will send for you.' " (Acts 24:25)

Some repented and believed. Some did not. All will stand before God for judgment.

LAWLESSNESS

As long as God is, there are some things that are good and some things that are bad. There are things that are permitted and others that are prohibited. The origin of the distinctions is the very nature of God. The distinctions do not come from His revelation to Israel at Sinai. They are included in it. These aspects of the nature of God are imprinted in all that He has made. This is the law of God.

Some people say that they do not have to obey the law of God, it does not apply to them. They claim to live in a lawless world. They are mistaken, for God will bring every thought, word, and deed into judgment. He will judge according to His law. "For since the creation of the world His invisible attributes, His eternal power and divine nature have been clearly seen, being understood through what has been made, so that they are without excuse." (Rom.1:20)

What do the New Covenant scriptures say about those who live as though there were no law of God to obey? The simplest way to find out is to look at the verses where the Greek word *anomian*, i.e. lawlessness, appears.

1John 3:4 equates living without the Law of God with living in sin. "Everyone who sins breaks the law; in fact, sin is **lawlessness**."

Messiah is described as one who hates lawlessness. In fact, it is because Messiah loves righteousness and hates lawlessness that God has chosen and anointed him. "But about the Son He says, 'Your throne, O God, will last for ever and ever, and righteousness will be the scepter of your kingdom. You have loved righteousness and hated **lawlessness**;

therefore God, your God, has set you above your companions by anointing you with the oil of joy.' " (Hebrews 1:8,9, quoting Ps.45:6-7, vv.7-8 in Hebrew)

Adam was created to live in obedience to God. Adam did not do that, nor did his descendants. Yeshua did. Because he did that, his throne and kingdom are established forever. If he had not done that, he would not have been righteous, and faith in him would be worthless, It is his righteousness that is the basis for salvation in him.

When Yeshua returns to set up the Messianic kingdom, his character will be exactly the same. He will still love righteousness and hate lawlessness. He will still live in accordance with the law of God.

Lot lived in the midst of Sodom, a city whose inhabitants hated righteousness. Lot, "living among them day after day, was tormented in his righteous soul by the lawless deeds [anomoi ergoi] he saw and heard." (2Pet. 2:8)

The inhabitants of Sodom had not been given the Law of Moses, but they still knew what God required of them. "Indeed, when Gentiles, who do not have the Law [of Moses], do by nature things required by the Law, they are a law for themselves, even though they do not have the Law, since they show that the requirements of the Law are written on their hearts, their consciences also bearing witness, and their thoughts now accusing, now even defending them." (Rom. 2:14-15)

They cannot escape from what God has put in their hearts and consciences. In the New Covenant, "the goal of our commandment is love from a pure heart and a good conscience and a sincere faith." 1Tim.1:5 God has commanded these things.

All disciples of Yeshua are also to hate and turn

away from living in opposition to God's Law. "Don't go on presenting the members of your body to sin as instruments of unrighteousness but present yourselves to God as those alive from the dead, your members as instruments of righteousness to God....I'm speaking in human terms because of the weakness of your flesh for just as you presented your members as slaves to impurity and **lawlessness** resulting in **lawlessness** so do the opposite now.....But now that you have been set free from sin and have become slaves to God, the benefit you reap leads to holiness, and the result is eternal life." (Rom.6:14,19,22)

Disciples of Yeshua are to "do the opposite" of lawlessness. The mind set on the flesh is hostile to God, i.e. it does not subject itself to the law of God. The mind set on the Spirit is the opposite of the mind set on the flesh.

As Paul explains, "Those who live according to the flesh set their minds on the things of the flesh; but those who live in accordance with the Spirit set their minds on the things of the Spirit. For the mind set on the flesh is death, but the mind set on the Spirit is life and peace; because the mind set on the flesh is hostile to God, for it does not subject itself to the law of God, for it is not even able to do so. And those who are in the flesh cannot please God." (Rom. 8:5-8)

When Yeshua speaks of the last days, he characterizes them as a time when more and more people reject God's Law, and the resultant ungodliness will quench the love of many. "Because of the increase of **lawlessness**, the love of most will grow cold." (Matt. 24:12)

In speaking about the time of judgment, Yeshua

said, "Not everyone who says to me, 'Lord, Lord,' will enter the kingdom of heaven, but only he who does the will of my Father who is in heaven. Many will say to me on that day, 'Lord, Lord did we not prophesy in your name and in your name cast out demons and in your name perform many miracles,' and then I will declare to them 'I never knew you. Depart from me you who practice **lawlessness**.' " (Matt 7:21-23)

He will not deny that they cast out demons or that they performed miracles. He will simply say, "I never knew you because you lived as though there were no Law of God." "...For what do righteousness and **lawlessness** have in common? Or what fellowship can light have with darkness?" (2Cor. 6:14)

"Therefore just as the tares are gathered up and burned with fire so shall it be at the end of the age. The son of Adam will send forth his angels and they will gather out of his kingdom all stumbling blocks and those who commit **lawlessness** and will cast them into the furnace of fire. In that place there shall be weeping and gnashing of teeth. Then the righteous will shine forth as the sun in the kingdom of their father. He who has ears let him hear." (Matt 13:40,41)

Yeshua is speaking about the consequences of how a person chooses to live. Those who choose to live as though there is no Law of God will be cast into the furnace of fire. They will be cast out of his kingdom into a place where there will be weeping and gnashing of teeth. This is a judgment especially for hypocrites, i.e. those who profess to know and serve the Lord, but deny him by their actions.

God "will give to each person according to what he has done. To those who by persistence in doing good seek glory, honor and immortality, He will give eternal life. But for those who are self-seeking and who reject the truth and follow evil, there will be wrath and anger." (Rom. 2:6-8)

Messiah loves the Law of God, and so do those who follow him. As Paul wrote, "I joyfully agree with the Law of God in my inner being." (Rom.7:22) Yeshua said, "Do not think that I came to abolish the Law or the Prophets; I did not come to abolish, but to establish." (Mt.5:17)

Yeshua did not come to do away with the Law of God, he came to establish it. It is the "Antichrist", the enemy of Messiah who proclaims a world free from God's law.

"Let no one in any way deceive you for it (the day of the Lord) will not come unless the falling away comes first and the man of **lawlessness** is revealed, the son of destruction....For the mystery of **lawlessness** is already at work only he who now restrains will do so until he is taken out of the way and then that lawless one will be revealed whom the Lord will slay with the breath of his mouth and bring to an end by the appearance of his coming. That is the one whose coming is in accord with the activity of Satan with all power and signs and false wonders and with all the deception of wickedness for those who perish because they did not receive the love of the truth so as to be saved." (2 Thes. 2:3,7-10)

The one who seeks to destroy the Law of God comes in the power of Satan. He is not the Messiah, but the antichrist. That's why "He who turns away his ear from listening to the Law, even his prayer is an abomination." (Prov.28:9)

Irenaeus was a second century Gentile believer, the disciple of Polycarp, the disciple of John. As a Gentile, he did not follow the Law of Moses. But he condemned as heretics all those who maintained that the Law had passed away.

"For all those who are of a perverse mind, having been set against the Mosaic legislation judging it to be dissimilar and contrary to the doctrine of the gospel, have not applied themselves to investigate the causes of the differences of each covenant. Since, therefore, they have been deserted by the paternal love, and puffed up by Satan, being brought over to the doctrine of Simon Magus, they have apostatized in their opinions from Him who is God, and imagined that they have themselves discovered more than the apostles, by finding out another God; and [have imagined] that the apostles preached the gospel still somewhat under the influence of Jewish opinions, but that they themselves are purer and more intelligent than the apostles."[1]

Judgment came upon Israel time and time again for turning away from God's law. "The LORD said, 'It is because they have forsaken My law, which I set before them; they have not obeyed Me or followed My law.' " (Jer. 9:13)

The purpose of atonement is to bring forgiveness for sin, not to make sin permissable. Yeshua redeemed us so that we would live holy lives, not so that we could continue to turn away from God's law. He redeemed us so that we could fulfill it, even as he did.

FOOTNOTE
1. Ante-Nicene Christian Library, Vol.5/1, trans. by A. Roberts and J. Donaldson, T & T Clark, Edinburgh, 1867, P.309

THE ALIEN IN THE LAND

The Law of Moses is not simply "religious" law, it is national law. It is law that was fully in force when Israel was sovereign, not under foreign domination. Therefore, Gentiles who chose to live in the land of Israel during such times had a different relationship to the Law of Moses than other Gentiles did.

That difference can be seen in the laws governing the feasts of the Lord, including Shabbat, the sacrifices in the Temple, purity, and sin. It can also be seen in the laws governing the practical means of loving one's neighbor as oneself. Significant parts of the Law of Moses were binding on Gentiles who lived in the midst of Israel. They were not Jews, but they were living in the land God had set apart for the Jews.

The Feasts of the Lord

Concerning Passover, the Lord declared, "For seven days no yeast is to be found in your houses. And whoever eats anything with yeast in it must be cut off from the community of Israel, whether he is an **alien** or native-born." (Exod. 12:19)

"An **alien** living among you who wants to celebrate the LORD's Passover must have all the males in his household circumcised; then he may take part like one born in the land. No uncircumcised male may eat of it. The same law applies to the native-born and to the **alien** living among you." (Exod. 12:48-49)

" 'An **alien** living among you who wants to celebrate the LORD's Passover must do so in accordance with its rules and regulations. You must have the same regulations for the **alien** and the native-born.' " (Num. 9:14)

As for Yom Kippur, "This is to be a lasting ordinance for you: On the tenth day of the seventh month you must deny yourselves and not do any work —whether native-born or an **alien** living among you — because on this day atonement will be made for you, to cleanse you. Then, before the LORD, you will be clean from all your sins. It is a sabbath of rest, and you must deny yourselves; it is a lasting ordinance." (Lev. 16:29-31)

In the same way, the blessing of Shabbat was for all. "The seventh day is a Sabbath to the LORD your God. On it you shall not do any work, neither you, nor your son or daughter, nor your manservant or maidservant, nor your animals, nor the **alien** within your gates." (Exod. 20:10)

"Six days do your work, but on the seventh day do not work, so that your ox and your donkey may rest and the slave born in your household, and the **alien** as well, may be refreshed." (Exod. 23:12)

"The seventh day is a Sabbath to the LORD your God. On it you shall not do any work, neither you, nor your son or daughter, nor your manservant or maidservant, nor your ox, your donkey or any of your animals, nor the **alien** within your gates, so that your manservant and maidservant may rest, as you do." (Deut. 5:14)

The sacrifices in the Temple

The laws covering sacrifices applied equally to all. "Say to them: 'Any of the children of Israel or any **alien** living among them who offers a burnt offering or sacrifice and does not bring it to the entrance to the Tent of Meeting to sacrifice it to the LORD —that man must be cut off from his people." (Lev. 17:8-9)

"Speak to Aaron and his sons and to all the children of Israel and say to them: 'If any of you — either one of the children of Israel or an **alien** living in Israel —presents a gift for a burnt offering to the LORD, either to fulfill a vow or as a freewill offering, you must present a male without defect from the cattle, sheep or goats in order that it may be accepted on your behalf. Do not bring anything with a defect, because it will not be accepted on your behalf.' " (Lev. 22:18-20)

"For the generations to come, whenever an **alien** or anyone else living among you presents an offering made by fire as an aroma pleasing to the LORD, he must do exactly as you do. The community is to have the same rules for you and for the **alien** living among you; this is a lasting ordinance for the generations to come. You and the **alien** shall be the same before the LORD: The same laws and regulations will apply both to you and to the **alien** living among you." (Num. 15:14-16)

Purity and Sin

The same was true for laws governing eating blood or the flesh of animals from which the blood had not been properly drained. "Any of the children of Israel or any **alien** living among you who eats any blood —I will set my face against that person who eats blood and will cut him off from his people. For the life of a creature is in the blood, and I have given it to you to make atonement for yourselves on the altar; it is the blood that makes atonement for one's life. Therefore I say to the children of Israel, 'None of you may eat blood, nor may an **alien** living among you eat blood.'

"Any of the children of Israel or any **alien** living

among you who hunts any animal or bird that may be eaten must drain out the blood and cover it with earth, because the life of every creature is its blood. That is why I have said to the children of Israel, 'You must not eat the blood of any creature, because the life of every creature is its blood; anyone who eats it must be cut off.'

"Anyone, whether native-born or **alien**, who eats anything found dead or torn by wild animals must wash his clothes and bathe with water, and he will be ceremonially unclean till evening; then he will be clean."[1] (Lev. 17:10-15)

Everyone had to treat the name of the Lord as holy. "Anyone who blasphemes the name of the LORD must be put to death. The entire assembly must stone him. Whether an **alien** or native-born, when he blasphemes the Name, he must be put to death." (Lev. 24:16)

No one was permitted to engage in the abominations for which God had destroyed the Canaanites. "Say to the children of Israel: 'Any of the children of Israel or any **alien** living in Israel who gives any of his children to Molech must be put to death. The people of the community are to stone him.' " (Lev. 20:2)

In general, sin was sin, no matter who committed it. "If anyone injures his neighbor, whatever he has done must be done to him: fracture for fracture, eye for eye, tooth for tooth. As he has injured the other, so he is to be injured. Whoever kills an animal must make restitution, but whoever kills a man must be put to death. You are to have the same law for the **alien** and the native-born. I am the LORD your God.' " (Lev. 24:19-22)

61

"One and the same law applies to everyone who sins unintentionally, whether he is a native-born of the children of Israel or an **alien**. But anyone who sins defiantly, whether native-born or **alien**, blasphemes the LORD, and that person must be cut off from his people." (Num. 15:29-30)

Provisions of Mercy

Even as the Gentiles living in the land were subject to the prohibitions that governed the life of the nation, so also they were the recipients of the mercy which God commanded. "Do not deprive the **alien** or the fatherless of justice, or take the cloak of the widow as a pledge." (Deut. 24:17)

"When you have finished setting aside a tenth of all your produce in the third year, the year of the tithe, you shall give it to the Levite, the **alien**, the fatherless and the widow, so that they may eat in your towns and be satisfied. Then say to the LORD your God: 'I have removed from my house the sacred portion and have given it to the Levite, the **alien**, the fatherless and the widow, according to all You commanded. I have not turned aside from your commandments nor have I forgotten any of them.' " (Deut. 26:12-13)

God instituted the provision of cities of refuge so that vengeance and blood feuds would not become the law of the land. "Any of the children of Israel or any **alien** living among them who killed someone accidentally could flee to these designated cities and not be killed by the avenger of blood prior to standing trial before the assembly." (Josh. 20:9)

And in the age to come, when Israel comes into the fulness of its inheritance, the Gentiles who have chosen to live within Israel will receive their portion as well. "You are to distribute this land among yourselves according to the tribes of Israel. You are to allot it as an inheritance for yourselves and for the **aliens** who have settled among you and who have children. You are to consider them as native-born children of Israel ; along with you they are to be allotted an inheritance among the tribes of Israel. In whatever tribe the **alien** settles, there you are to give him his inheritance,' declares the Sovereign LORD." (Ezek. 47:21-23) They live according to the law of the land, and have their inheritance in the land.

It is also worth noting that during the first century there were many Gentiles who were not proselytes who habitually attended synagogue in the Diaspora. They were seeking God, and the synagogue was the only place where His Word was proclaimed. They did not become Jews, but they adopted many Jewish customs and practices. At different times, this caused them great problems with the Roman government. When these God-fearers believed in Yeshua, they continued in their observances.

FOOTNOTE
1. Deut. 14:21 seems to modify Lev.17:15: "Do not eat anything you find already dead. You may give it to an **alien** who is within your gates, and he may eat it, or you may sell it to a foreigner...." Because of this and other verses, the Rabbis saw distinctions being made between the *ger ha'sha'ar* (the Gentile within the gate), the *ger toshav* (the Gentile fully living with the people), and the *ger tzedek* (the Gentile who became a proselyte).

GOD'S LAW IN THE DAYS TO COME

"Now it will come about in the last days that the mountain of the house of the Lord will be established as the chief of the mountains and will be raised above the hills. And all the nations (goyim, Gentiles) will stream to it. And many peoples will say 'Come let us go up to the mountain of the Lord to the house of the God of Jacob that He may teach us concerning his ways and that we may walk in his paths.' For torah (law, teaching) will go forth from Zion and the word of the Lord from Jerusalem. And He will judge between the nations (goyim) and will render decisions for many peoples. And they will hammer their swords into plowshares and their spears into pruning hooks. Nation will not lift up sword against nation and never again will they learn war." (Is.2:2-4; Mic.4:1-3)

In the days to come, God will judge the goyim on the basis of the particular torah that then goes forth from Zion. God's kingdom will be established upon the earth with Jerusalem as its capital. All the peoples of the earth will come to Jerusalem to learn the ways of righteousness. "Her ways are ways of pleasantness, and all her paths are peace." (Prov. 3:17)

This has been God's plan from the beginning. He created Israel to be a light to the nations. As Yeshua commanded his Jewish disciples, "Go into all the earth making disciples of all the Gentiles...and teach them all that I have commanded you." (Mt.28:19-20) Teach them Messiah's law. As Paul said, quoting from Isaiah the prophet, "For this is what the Lord has commanded us, 'I have set you as a light for the Gentiles, that you should bring salvation to the end of the earth.' " (Acts 13:47)

God asked Jonah to do the same. "Go to the great city of Nineveh and preach against it, because its wickedness has come up before me." (Jonah 1:2) The wickedness of the Gentile city of Nineveh was great. So God told Jonah to go there and preach. Jonah wanted to escape this aspect of his calling as a Jew, but God would not let him.

With repentance and faith, the Gentiles can enter into Israel's New Covenant through the King of the Jews. " 'The time is coming,' declares the LORD, 'when I will make a new covenant with the house of Israel and with the house of Judah. It will not be like the covenant I made with their forefathers when I took them by the hand to lead them out of Egypt, because they broke My covenant, though I was a husband to them,' declares the LORD. 'This is the covenant I will make with the house of Israel after that time,' declares the LORD. 'I will put My law in their minds and write it on their hearts. I will be their God, and they will be My people.' " (Jer. 31:31-33; Heb.8:8-12)

It is this New Covenant, the only new covenant mentioned in the Bible, that brings righteousness to Israel and to the goyim. The context is God's faithfulness to Israel, despite our centuries of breaking His law. TheNew Covenant is characterized by the law of God being written on the hearts and minds of all who enter into it.

In speaking of the day when He will comfort Zion, the Lord says, "Listen to Me you who pursue righteousness, who seek the Lord... Listen to Me, My people; hear Me, My nation: For torah will go forth from Me; My justice will become a light to the peoples....Listen to Me you who know righteousness, you who have My law in your hearts. My

65

righteousness is near, My salvation has gone forth and My arm will bring justice to the nations. The coastlands will wait for Me and for My arm they will wait expectantly." (Is.51:1-7)

In these verses, God equates pursuing righteousness with seeking the Lord. He equates knowing righteousness with having His law in our hearts. When His law is accepted in the hearts of the peoples, then there will be justice in the earth.

It is the "arm" of the Lord that brings God's law to the nations, bringing justice and light to all the earth. The "arm of the Lord," as in Isaiah 53, refers to Messiah.

There is a parallel portion in Isaiah 42 that speaks explicitly of Messiah. "Behold My servant whom I uphold, My chosen one in whom My soul delights. I have put My spirit upon him. He will bring forth justice to the Gentiles. He will not cry out or raise his voice nor make his voice heard in the street. A bruised reed he will not break and a dimly burning wick he will not extinguish. He will faithfully bring forth justice. He will not be disheartened or crushed until he has established justice in the earth and the coastlands will wait expectantly for his torah." (Is. 42:1-4)

The coastlands wait for the Lord, and they wait for the torah of His servant. In Messiah, Israel can fulfill the prophetic calling to teach the goyim what God requires of them. They need to receive "his torah." What is the nature of the torah that goes forth from Zion to the Gentiles? To know that, we need to first understand the nature of the torah that God gave to Israel.

The Torah tells us that God made the Gentiles (Gen. 11) before He called Abraham (Gen. 12). Abram was a Gentile. God called him, and then created Israel, because the Gentiles were hopelessly lost in sin. God had given the Gentiles His unwritten law in their consciences, but He did not give the Law of Moses to the Gentiles.

God established a covenant with Abraham, Isaac, Jacob, and their descendants. He gave the Law of Moses to those descendants as a specific revelation of His righteousness and holiness. It contains concrete commandments for loving and serving Him and for loving one's neighbor as oneself. "All the Law and the Prophets depend on these two commandments." (Mt.22:40) The Law of Moses contained provisions both to set Israel apart from the nations in holiness, and also to lead us to Messiah, so that we could bring the nations back to God.

God's covenant relationship with Israel was established before the Law of Moses was given. Redemption from Egypt preceded the giving of the law at Sinai. Living in accordance with God's law is not the means of redemption, it is the goal or fruit of it.

People sometimes divide the law of God into "moral," "civil," and "ceremonial" categories. Some then say that the "moral" law of God still stands, the "civil" law was for the nation of Israel only, and the "ceremonial" law has passed away. These categories can be helpful, but the text of the Torah itself can not always be easily conformed to them.

If the "moral" law governs only man's relationship with his fellow man, and not man's relationship with God, then the first four of the Ten Commandments, including the prohibition of idolatry, cannot be considered part of the "moral" law. (cf. Ex. 20:1-11) They deal with man's relationship with God. If, on the other hand, man's relationship with God is considered part of the "moral law", then all of Torah is "moral law", because all of Torah is commanded by God and is part of man's relationship with Him.

Much that is contained in the law of Moses was already required of all people. Throughout the Bible we can see that God held the Gentiles accountable for all the 10 Commandments except Shabbat. The observance of Shabbat is a covenant sign between God and Israel forever. (Ex.31:16-17)

Nevertheless, the Lord says, "Blessed is the man who...keeps the Sabbath without desecrating it, and keeps his hand from doing any evil." This includes both Jew and Gentile. (Is.56:1-7)

In the ages to come, everyone will observe Shabbat. " 'As the new heavens and the new earth that I make will endure before me,' declares the LORD, 'so will your name and descendants endure. From one New Moon to another and from one Sabbath to another, all mankind will come and bow down before Me,' says the LORD." (Is. 66:22-23).

In the Scriptures we can also see that God held the Gentiles guilty for sins of violence and sexual immorality. That was and is part of the law that He has given to them. (See the section "Are Non-Jews without Law?")

It is likewise difficult to differentiate the "civil" law from the "moral" law, because the "civil" law also regulates the way a man should treat his neighbor. There are specifics in the "civil law" in Torah that require a theocracy in the land of Israel. In that respect, the "civil" law is given to Israel only, but it is still the model for all nations. All nations need to acknowledge the sovereignty of God.

Moses said, "See I have taught you statutes and judgments just as the Lord my God commanded me that you should do thus in the land where you're entering to possess it. So keep and do them for that is your wisdom and your understanding in the sight of the peoples who will hear all these statutes and say, 'Surely this great nation is a wise and understanding people,' for what great nation is there that has a God so near to it as is the Lord our God whenever we call on him or what great nation is there that has statutes and judgments as righteous as this whole law which I am setting before you today." (Dt. 4:5-8) God's whole law is righteous, giving wisdom to whoever will receive it.

As for the "ceremonial" law, we have already seen that Shabbat will be observed in the ages to come. It was given to Israel as an eternal covenant to commemorate God's creation of the world. During the time in the wilderness, God commanded that a man who refused to observe Shabbat be put to death. (Num.15:32-36) That is a rather severe punishment for breaking a merely "ceremonial" law. God considers it very important.

God rested from His labors and made Shabbat holy. To live wholly in God's image. man needs to do the same. "The Sabbath was made for man, and not man for the Sabbath." (Mk.2:27)

Yeshua celebrated Passover, the feast of redemption, with his disciples. He took the cup after supper and told them, "I will not drink of this again until the kingdom of God comes." (Lk.22:18) He will drink of that cup again when the kingdom of God fills the earth. He will celebrate Passover.

The same is true of Sukkot. In the age to come all the nations will come to Jerusalem to celebrate

Sukkot, the feast of tabernacles. "Then it will come about that any who are left of all the Gentiles who went against Jerusalem will go up from year to year to worship the King, the Lord of hosts, and to celebrate the feast of tabernacles." (Zech.14:16)

This refers to a time when the Lord has descended and his feet have stood upon the Mt. of Olives. It is after He has destroyed all those who sought to destroy Jerusalem. This is after the return of the Lord.

At that time, "whichever of the families of the earth does not go up to Jerusalem to worship the King, the Lord of hosts, there will be no rain on them. And if the family of Egypt does not go up or enter then no rain will fall on them. It will be the plague with which the Lord smites the goyim who do not go up to celebrate Sukkot. This will be the punishment of Egypt and the punishment of all the goyim who do not go up to celebrate Sukkot." (Zech.14:17-19)

God proclaims a death sentence, i.e. no rain, for any nation that will not come to Jerusalem to celebrate Sukkot before Him in Jerusalem. There is no other way to understand the text. God considers it very important.

Additionally, in the Messianic age the priests will again offer sacrifices on the altar in the Temple. This is described in Ezekiel chapters 40 through 46. We may not understand or appreciate the reinstitution of the sacrifices, but the text itself is clear that it will happen.

Inasmuch as the law of God is a reflection of who God is, the law does not and cannot pass away. All torah, however, must be understood in its context, because it is also a reflection of who man is.

First, some laws are only applicable for some

people in certain circumstances. For the most part, such laws are gender-specific, time specific, place-specific, or people-specific. Some laws concerning purification, for example, apply to women and not to men. Some apply to men and not to women.

Some laws apply only to a certain day or year, or time of year. Some apply only to a certain time of life, e.g. birth, maturity, marriage, war, or death.

The laws governing the exclusion of lepers, or their readmittance to the community if healed, apply only to lepers. The laws governing the treatment of slaves only apply to those who have slaves. The laws do not pass away, but if you do not have slaves, they do not apply to you.

There are laws that only apply when the people of Israel are living in the land of Israel in a sovereign state. Israel is not commanded to set up cities of refuge in the diaspora, or to destroy all the idolatrous places of worship. All the laws concerning the Temple, its functions, and the priesthood are contingent upon the people of Israel being in the land of Israel under the God of Israel.

Then there are the laws that are people-specific. They apply to the Jewish people. God commands these things of Israel because Israel, as a people set apart, is to represent God in the earth.

" 'You are My witnesses,' declares the LORD, 'and My servant whom I have chosen, so that you may know and believe Me and understand that I am He. Before Me no god was formed, nor will there be one after Me. I, even I, am the LORD, and apart from Me there is no savior. I have revealed and saved and proclaimed — I, and not some foreign god among you. You are My witnesses,' declares the LORD, 'that I am God.' " (Is. 43:10-12)

By observing Shabbat, Israel commemorates and bears witness of God's creation and ownership of all that is. By wearing fringes, by binding God's Word on our hands and between our eyes, by writing them upon the doorposts of our houses and our gates, Israel testifies that God's Word is the only acceptable rule of life. By not eating unclean animals, and by not mixing different kinds of seeds, Israel bears witness that God differentiates, choosing the clean and rejecting the unclean. (See the section on Difficult Passages.)

Second, for both Jews and Gentiles there are changes that take place when the law that God has given us is written on our hearts. It becomes second nature to us. It is no longer an external standard that we strive to attain, but a life that proceeds from the Spirit of God within us.

God promises that when we enter into the New Covenant, "I will give you a new heart and put a new spirit in you; I will remove from you your heart of stone and give you a heart of flesh. And I will put My Spirit in you and cause you to follow My statutes and be careful to keep My ordinances. You will live in the land I gave your forefathers; you will be My people, and I will be your God." (Ezek.36:26-28) Through the New Covenant, God puts His law, His statutes and ordinances, and His Spirit in the hearts of His people.

The law on our hearts requires more from us. Yeshua explained that when "You shall not murder" is written on our hearts, we are also forbidden to hate, as God had commanded in Lev.19:17. Even more than that, he said, "I tell you that anyone who is angry with his brother will be subject to judgment. Again, anyone who says to his brother, 'Raca,' is answerable to the Sanhedrin. But anyone who says, 'You fool!' will be in danger of the fire of hell." (Mt.5:22)

Yeshua also explained that when "You shall not commit adultery" is written on our hearts, we are also forbidden to lust. (cf. Mt.5:17-32) The external prohibition is maintained and extended to include the thoughts and desires of the heart, which are what lead to the unrighteous action. A pure heart was always God's desire for mankind.

In seeking to love and serve God, Moses lived according to God's law. So did all the men and women in Tanakh with whom God was pleased. Through the prophets, God denounced Israel and the nations for turning away from His law.

As the Messiah, Yeshua is **THE** example of a life pleasing to God. He lived according to the Law of Moses. So did Paul and all the Jewish apostles and disciples.

Yeshua said that he came to establish the law. (Mt.5:17) Paul said that faith in Yeshua does not nullify the law, but, on the contrary, establishes it. Literally, "through faith, we cause the law to stand." (Rom.3:31) Paul explained that the reason for Yeshua's atoning death is that the righteous requirement of the law might be fulfilled in us. (Rom.8:4) In the days to come, that righteous living will be a visible reality.

The Lord promised Israel blessings for fulfilling the Law, and curses for rejecting it. Exile from the land and terror living among the nations was the ultimate judgment. Nevertheless, God promised that after all these things He would bring us back to the land He promised to our fathers. (Dt. 30:1-5)

Then, Moses declared, "The LORD your God will circumcise your hearts and the hearts of your

73

descendants, to love the Lord your God with all your heart and with all your soul, that you may live.... You will again obey the LORD and observe all His commandments which I command you this day." (Dt. 30:6, 8)

Circumcision of the heart leads to the observance of God's commandments.

Third, there are priorities and accomodations within God's law. The priests worked in the Temple on Shabbat. The high priest worked on the Day of Atonement. A baby boy is to be circumcised on the eighth day, even if it is Shabbat. Those who are unclean at Passover because of the dead can celebrate it a month later. (Num. 9)

Jewish history and tradition show a recognition of these priorities. The Maccabees decided to fight on Shabbat, rather than be slaughtered, because the law of God was given that we might live by it. For the preservation of life, it was deemed necessary and permissable to break Shabbat.

When Rabban Gamaliel was elderly and ill, his wife died. Because of his illness he did not observe the rabbinic laws of mourning which he himself had taught. He "bathed on the first night after his wife died. His disciples said to him, 'Didn't you teach us that a mourner is forbidden to bathe?' He said to them, 'I am not like others. I am not well.' " (Berakhot 2:6) For the preservation of life, his illness was seen to justify an accomodation.

Within Torah itself, and throughout Tanakh, God indicates that some changes in the law will take place in the Messianic age. The Rabbis also recognized that there would be differences. That is the focus of the next section on "Differences Between the Covenants".

74

DIFFERENCES BETWEEN THE COVENANTS

The early Rabbis and other Jews of two thousand years ago recognized that there would be changes in the Law of God in the Messianic age, when the New Covenant would be fully in force. Messiah himself was seen as the authoritative interpreter of Torah who would explain the differences between the covenants. Whatever he taught was to be obeyed.

Moses had prophesied that, "The LORD your God will raise up for you a prophet like me from among your own brothers. You must listen to him. For this is what you asked of the LORD your God at Horeb on the day of the assembly when you said, 'Let us not hear the voice of the LORD our God nor see this great fire anymore, or we will die.'

"The LORD said to me: 'What they say is good. I will raise up for them a prophet like you from among their brothers; I will put My words in his mouth, and he will tell them everything I command him. If anyone does not listen to My words that the prophet speaks in My name, I Myself will call him to account.'" (Deut. 18:15-19)

The Talmud says of Messiah, "Come and hear: *Unto him ye shall hearken*, even if he tells you, 'Transgress any of all the commandments of the Torah' as in the case, for instance, of Elijah on Mount Carmel, obey him in every respect in accordance with the needs of the hour!" (Yebamot 90b)

The Torah ends with a reminder of God's promise to send Messiah: "Since then, no prophet has risen in Israel like Moses, whom the LORD knew face to face, who did all those miraculous signs and wonders the LORD sent him to do in Egypt —to Pharaoh and to all his officials and to his whole land. For no one has ever shown the mighty power or performed the awesome deeds that Moses did in the sight of all Israel." (Dt. 34:10-12)

The implication is that Messiah would be the prophet who would, like Moses, perform miraculous signs and wonders, destroy the power of the oppressor, and redeem Israel. And, like Moses, he would present God's Law to the people.

In the Dead Sea scrolls from Qumran, especially in the "Rule of the Community", Messiah is presented as the final interpreter of God's Torah. (e.g. 1QS 3.13 & 4QFlor.1:11-12) To some extent, this same role had also been anticipated in 1 Maccabees, concerning the cleansing of the altar which had been defiled. (1Mac.4:46)

Some rabbis expected Torah to change in the days of Messiah. The rabbinic Midrash on Psalms suggests that unclean animals may be declared clean. "Some say that in the time to come all the animals which are unclean in this world God will declare to be clean, as they were in days before Noah. And why did God forbid them? To see who would accept his bidding and who would not; but in the time to come He will permit all that He has forbidden." (Mid. Teh. 146:7)

In the Talmud, the Rabbis even say that, "In the days of the Messiah, bastards [i.e. the children of forbidden marriages]...will be pure." (Kid.72b) 2 Baruch speaks of the inclusion in the covenant community of Gentiles who observe God's law, and the exclusion of Jews who do not.

Other rabbinic writings refer to a new Torah that is related to the Torah given at Sinai but different in some respects. "The Holy One, blessed be He, will sit in Paradise and give instruction, and all the righteous will sit before Him and all the hosts of Heaven will stand on His right and the sun, and stars on His left; and the Holy One, blessed be He, interprets to them the grounds of a new Torah which the Holy One, blessed be He, will give to them by the hand of King Messiah." (Yalqut on Is.26)

The Rabbis pondered the relationship of the dead to Torah, since the dead are to be resurrected with the coming of Messiah. (cf. Sotah 48b, Gen. Rab.96:5) Once a person has died, is he still obligated to observe all the laws? The Rabbis concluded that those who died were free from the commandments.[1]

However, freedom from the commandments, either through death or the resurrection, did not mean lawlessness or the freedom to disobey God. Rather, the Rabbis believed that in the days of Messiah, "Man's deeds will be spontaneously good." (Lev. Rab.18:1 n.5, citing Eccl.12:1)

This is much the same as what Paul wrote: "Do you not know brethren — for I am speaking to men who know the law — that the law has authority over a man only as long as he lives?" (Rom.7:1) For those of us who are Jewish, our failure to keep the Law of Moses condemns us to God's judgment of death. In Messiah we are put to death, as the Law requires. Paul then explained that the new life which one receives in the resurrection of Messiah produces righteousness by its very nature, not by any obligation to the Law. It is not the Law which dies, it is the transgressor of the Law who dies.

In Tanakh, there is a basis for these expectations. In promising to make a New Covenant, God said that it would be different from the covenant made at Sinai, but would still have His Law at the center. The text of the New Covenant promise indicates the differences and changes from the Covenant of the Law.

" 'The time is coming,' declares the LORD, 'when I will make a new covenant with the house of Israel and with the house of Judah. It will not be like the covenant I made with their forefathers when I took them by the hand to lead them out of Egypt, because they broke My covenant, though I was a husband to them,' declares the LORD.

" 'This is the covenant I will make with the house of Israel after that time,' declares the LORD. 'I will put My law in their minds and write it on their hearts. I will be their God, and they will be My people. No longer will a man teach his neighbor, or a man his brother, saying, Know the LORD, because they will all know Me, from the least of them to the greatest,' declares the LORD. 'For I will forgive their wickedness and will remember their sins no more.' " (Jer. 31:31-34)

God said that the New Covenant would be different from the covenant of the law made at Sinai. His purpose did not change, but Israel broke the covenant of the law made at Sinai, resulting in judgment. Through the new covenant, with its differences, God intends to bring Israel into a righteous relationship with Himself. The nature of the differences between the Covenant of the Law and the New Covenant is contained in God's three prophetic declarations:

1. "I will put My law in their minds and write it on their hearts."

2. "I will be their God, and they will be My people."

3. "I will forgive their wickedness and will

remember their sins no more."

1. "I will put My law in their minds and write it on their hearts."

In the covenant made at Sinai, God had included certain symbolic practices to remind Israel to think about and obey His Law. The mezuzah, tefillin, and tzitzit symbolize Israel's submission to God's Law. They serve as ever-present reminders to keep God's commandments on our hearts. (Dt.6:4-9)

As the Lord said of tzitzit, "Speak to the children of Israel and say to them: 'Throughout the generations to come you are to make fringes on the corners of your garments, with a blue thread on each fringe. You will have these fringes to look at that you may remember all the commandments of the LORD, that you may obey them and not prostitute yourselves by going after the lusts of your own hearts and eyes." (Num. 15:38-39)

The Rabbis say of tefillin, however, that since they are a sign to remind Israel of the commandments of God, they are not worn on Shabbat or the holy days because these days are a sufficient reminder in themselves. (cf. Eruvin 96a) "The very Sabbath day itself and the very festival itself is intended to serve as an everpresent reminder of God's Presence and of His commandments....To add the observance of tefillin in the context of its meaning and purpose would not only be superfluous but would imply downgrading the Sabbath."[2]

Unfortunately, although the symbols themselves remind us,[3] as do Shabbat and the festivals, they do not give us the power to keep the commandments, and they cannot produce submission in our hearts.

That is why, in the New Covenant, God puts His law in our minds and writes it on our hearts. The reminder comes from within.

Where does the power to live righteously come from? From God's Spirit living within. The Messianic Age, the age of the outpouring of God's Holy Spirit is characterized by holiness.

Israel and the world are transformed, and "In that day there will be upon the bells of horses: 'Holy unto the Lord;' and the posts in the Lord's house shall be like the basins before the altar. Yea, every pot in Jerusalem and in Judah shall be holy unto the Lord of hosts..." (Zech.14:20-21)

This is the core of God's second promise in the New Covenant He makes with Israel:

2. "I will be their God, and they will be My people."

God repeats this New Covenant promise in Ezekiel 37:27, after first promising: "I will give you a new heart and put a new spirit in you; I will remove from you your heart of stone and give you a heart of flesh. And I will put My Spirit in you and move you to follow My decrees and be careful to keep My laws."(Ezek. 36:26-27 cf 37:1-14)

God's Spirit provides the power to walk in accordance with His commandments. God gives His Spirit to those who enter into the New Covenant. His Spirit draws us into close relationship with Him, making us the people He has always wanted us to be.

The complete fulfillment of this promise takes place at the end of this age. As the Lord said in Zech.13:9, "... I will refine them like silver and test them like gold. The will call on My Name and I will answer them; I will say, 'They are My people,' and they will say, 'The Lord is our God.' "

Abraham, the father of the Jewish people, is a God-given example of the way we should walk before the Lord. (cf Is.51:1-2) He left his country, his relatives, and his father's house to follow God. He believed God for His promise of a supernaturally conceived son. He obediently put that son on the wood as a sacrifice to God, believing in His power to resurrect Isaac to fulfill His promise.

In all of this, we see that Abraham trusted, and therefore obeyed, God completely. "Abraham believed God and it was counted to him for righteousness." (Gen.15:6) Faith was the means by which Abraham was considered righteous by God, but it is not the sum and the end of that righteousness. Abraham's faith produced a very tangible deed when he offered up Isaac. (Gen. 22)

God considered Abraham righteous because of his faith, the internal decision of his heart. The righteousness of the law is different, as Moses told our ancestors: "And if we are careful to obey all this law before the LORD our God, as He has commanded us, that will be our righteousness." (Deut. 6:25)

The Biblical record demonstrates that we did not "obey all this law." Today, we are not better than our fathers. We need a different source of righteousness. In the New Covenant we believe as Abraham did, and we receive from God the same righteousness he received.

3. "I will forgive their wickedness and will remember their sins no more."

In the New Covenant, there is a difference in (a) the means of atonement, (b) the power of that atonement, (c) the priesthood which offers the sacrifice, and (d) the Temple in which the sacrifice is offered. Each of these is regulated by specific commandments in the Covenant of the Law.

God is therefore promising to change those specific commandments when He institutes the New Covenant. God indicated in Jer.31:31-34 that there would be all these differences between His New Covenant with Israel and the Covenant of the Law He made with us at Sinai.

How can God's law change? God created Adam without sin in a world without sin. When Adam chose to sin, however, he changed, the world changed, and so did his relationship with God. God Himself did not change, but His instruction to Adam did, because of Adam's changed nature and circumstances.

Initially God placed Adam in the garden of Eden and gave him the responsibility of taking care of it. (cf. Gen.2:15) When Adam rebelled against God, he was excluded from the garden and his responsibility changed.

In the same way, in the days to come, when Israel is a redeemed people, we and our circumstances will have changed. God's instruction for our relationship with Him will change accordingly, even as it did for Adam. His covenant with Abraham, the foundation for Israel's relationship with God, remains the same.

What are the differences in **(a) the means of atonement**?

In Torah, God had declared that it is the blood, i.e. the sacrificial death, of an innocent other that brings atonement. (Lev.17:11) Vicarious atonement, the death of an innocent other in the place of the guilty, is at the heart of the Covenant of the Law. In that covenant, however, sheep, bulls, and goats were the innocent others who were sacrificed. In the New

Covenant, it is Messiah.

Can one man atone for the sins of another? Can one man atone for the sins of all Israel? If God had not promised and declared it, there would be no reason to believe it. But He did promise it as His New Covenant way of removing our sin from us.

In Torah, God stipulated that a person who unintentionally killed another was to flee from the blood-avenger to a city of refuge and live there until the death of the High Priest. (Num. 35:22-28) The High Priest is called the Anointed One, *haCohen haMoshiach*. (e.g. Lev.4:3,5,16) The death of the High Priest cancelled any right of vengeance which the relatives of the one killed might have had. In effect, the death of the High Priest, the Anointed One, brought atonement. In the Talmud, the Rabbis also noted, "It is the death of the [high] priest that procures the atonement." (Mak.11b)

God commanded the sacrifice of Abraham's only son. (Gen.22) As Abraham prepared to sacrifice Isaac in obedience to God's command, he told Isaac that God Himself would provide the lamb for the sacrifice. In response to Abraham's obedience in offering his only son to be sacrificed, God declared Abraham worthy to be the father of all those from every nation who would be God's people.

On that day, however, God did **not** provide a lamb in place of Isaac. He provided a ram. The time when God would provide that promised lamb was still in the future. [In the traditional Yom Kippur liturgy, God is asked to remember the binding of Isaac as though it were the equivalent of the atoning sacrifices in the Temple.]

Isaiah the prophet spoke of Messiah as the ultimate atoning lamb: "But he was pierced for our transgressions, he was crushed for our iniquities; the punishment that brought us peace was upon him, and by his wounds we are healed. We all, like sheep, have gone astray, each of us has turned to his own way; and **the LORD has laid on him the iniquity of us all**. He was oppressed and he was afflicted, but he did not open his mouth; like **a lamb** that is led to slaughter, and like a sheep that is silent before its shearers, so he did not open his mouth...

"Yet it was the LORD's will to crush him putting him to grief. If he would render his soul as a **guilt offering**, he will see his offspring, he will prolong his days, and the good pleasure of the Lord will prosper in his hand. As a result of the anguish of his soul he will see the light of life and be satisfied. By his knowledge the righteous one My servant will justify the many as **he will bear their iniquities**. Therefore, I will allot him a portion with the great and he will divide the booty with the strong because he poured out his soul to death and was numbered with the transgressors yet **he himself bore the sin of many** and interceded for the transgressors." (Isa. 53:5-7,10-12)

This is a portion which the ancient rabbis as well as the followers of Yeshua understood to be speaking of Messiah. The Lord put Messiah to death as a guilt offering to atone for our sin, transgression, and iniquity.

(b) the power of that atonement: The covenant of the Law provided for ongoing sacrifices for ongoing sins. Each sin required another sacrifice. There was no end to the sacrifices because there was no end to the sins. Additionally, atonement could only be made for sins that had already been committed, not for sins that would be committed in the future.

In the New Covenant, the sacrifice of Messiah is not limited to one direction in time. One sacrifice atones for all sins, whether committed before or after that sacrifice is offered. The Messianic sacrifice brings more than atonement. It also brings peace, healing, and being acceptable to God.

David spoke prophetically for Messiah, his descendant: "Sacrifice and meal offering you have not desired. My ears you have opened. Burnt offering and sin offering you have not required. Then I said, 'Behold I come. In the scroll of the book it is written of me: *I delight to do your will, O my God. Your law is within my heart.*' "(Ps. 40:6-8)

In the Covenant of the Law, God did require burnt offerings and sin offerings. Messiah who comes with God's law within his heart, comes to do the will of God and, by offering himself, makes all other sacrifices unnecessary in and of themselves. They simply serve to teach of and point to the one sacrifice.

(c) the priesthood which offers the sacrifice: A Levitical priest cannot offer this kind of sacrifice. In Tanakh, however, God speaks of other priesthoods.

The Levites, after all, were chosen as substitutes for the first-born male of each family, the natural priest of each family. (Num.3:41) Before God chose the Levites, they were not the priests of Israel. Moses served as the priest of God in anointing Aaron and establishing his priesthood. (cf. Lev. 8:14-30) Moses was obviously not descended from his brother Aaron.

After the Levitical priesthood was chosen, there were times when God bypassed the order He had established for them. Eli is a case in point. He was God's high priest, but he did not raise his children to fear the Lord. God rebuked Eli for his immoral sons, and promised, "I will raise up for myself a faithful priest, who will do according to what is in My heart and mind. I will firmly establish his house, and he will minister before My anointed one always." (1Sam. 2:35) God chose Samuel to be His priest in the place of the sons of Eli.

Samuel served as God's high priest in anointing both Saul and then David as King of Israel. The promise that God would raise up "a faithful priest" referred to Samuel, but it looked beyond him to Messiah, a greater priest.

Samuel, after all, did not minister before either Saul or David always, literally "all the days," as God had promised. When Saul turned away from the Lord, Samuel turned away from Saul. And as for David, Samuel died before David ascended the throne.

God had commanded that when the Temple was built, all sacrifices should be offered there by the sons of Aaron. Elijah, who is not identified as a descendant of Aaron, offered sacrifices on Mt. Carmel in his confrontation with the prophets of Baal. God sent fire from heaven to complete the sacrifices and demonstrate that He was the only true God. (1Kings 18) God had chosen Elijah for that purpose.

Long before Elijah, Samuel, Aaron, or even Levi, God had already established a different priesthood. After a successful military rescue operation, Abraham gave a tenth of all the spoils to Melchizedek, "a priest of God Most High." (Gen.14:18-20). Melchizedek, whose name means "king of righteousness," was also the king of Salem. He was both a king and a priest.

Messiah belongs to the same priesthood. "The LORD will extend your mighty scepter from Zion; you will rule in the midst of your enemies. ...The Lord has sworn and will not change His mind. You are a priest forever according to the order of Melchizedek." (Ps.110:2,4) Like Melchizedek, Messiah is both a king and a priest.

In the covenant of the Law, from David on, the kings were to come from the tribe of Judah, and the priests from the tribe of Levi. No one could be both, even though all Israel was to be a kingdom of priests to bring the nations to God. (Ex.19:6)

Zechariah also prophesied of Messiah as a priest and a king. (Zech.6:11-13) The Lord told Zechariah to put an ornate crown on Yeshua, the high priest, and seat him on a throne. The Lord said that Yeshua represented Messiah who would be both priest and king.

Messiah is to be a priest like Samuel, doing all that is in God's heart and mind, and a king like David, a man after God's own heart. God promised to bring such a priest from the order of Melchizedek because the Levitical priests could not set the people free from sin. They could not set themselves free from sin.

(d) the Temple in which the New Covenant sacrifice is offered: The sacrifice of Messiah cannot be offered within the Temple confines or system. It would defile the Temple altar, rather than bring atonement. (cf. 2Kings 23:16) Yet it is this one sacrifice that establishes the New Covenant and atones for all the sins of those who enter into the covenant.

Following the giving of the Ten Commandments, God gave Israel instructions for the altars "in every place" on which they would offer sacrifices to Him. (cf. Exod. 20:22-26; vv19-23 in Heb.) He did not initially specify one place where sacrifices were to be offered to Him in the land of Israel. There would be many places. Later God designated one particular place.

Where could God receive the sacrifice of Messiah as an offering for sin, presented by a priest of the order of Melchizedek? God encompassed Moses in His glory and showed him the pattern for the Tabernacle he was to make. (Ex.24:15-25:9,40) God supernaturally revealed to David the plan for the Temple. (1Chr.28:19) In the visions of God, Ezekiel was shown the design of the third Temple.

God commanded that these places of worship and sacrifice be made exactly according to the pattern He revealed from heaven. He was present in their Holy of Holies, but earthly temples are inadequate to fully contain and reveal God's glory. They are also inadequate for the New Covenant sacrifice which brings complete atonement and forgiveness.

The Lord said to Israel, "Heaven is My throne, the earth is My footstool. Where then is the house you could build for Me and where is the place that I may rest. For My hand made all these things." (Is. 66:1) God is enthroned in the heavenly temple, which provided the pattern for the sanctuaries on earth. There is a heavenly Jerusalem. (e.g. Gal.4:26) The Rabbis also recognized that. (e.g. Ta'anit 5a)

The Lord warned Israel to trust in Him, and not in the Temple. "Do not trust in deceptive words and say, "This is the temple of the LORD, the temple of the LORD, the temple of the LORD!" (Jer. 7:4) In the Talmud, R. Joseph taught that this meant the first two temples would be destroyed because of Israel's sins and a third one built. (Naz.32b)

The Temple itself could not take away our sins. To the contrary, our sins took away the Temple. A place beyond the reach of our sins was necessary.

God spoke of a time of restoration when He

would dwell in our midst and Jerusalem would be called "The Throne of the LORD." "In those days, ...men will no longer say, 'The ark of the covenant of the LORD.' It will never enter their minds or be remembered; it will not be missed, nor will another one be made.' " (Jer. 3:16-17)

The ark, in the Holy of Holies, was the place where atonement was made for all Israel on Yom Kippur, the Day of Atonement. The fact that there will be no ark and that it will not be missed means that complete and final atonement will already have been made. Messiah, as a priest of the order of Melchizedek, will have entered the heavenly Holy of Holies to offer his own blood to secure our eternal redemption. (cf.Heb. 9:11-12)

FOOTNOTES

1. Torah prohibits the mixing of wool and linen in the garments worn by the Jewish people. (e.g. Dt.22:11-12) This and the other statutes which prohibit the mixing of different kinds of things, i.e. kil'ayim, are symbolic of the separation that God requires of Israel.

"Our Rabbis taught: A garment in which kil'ayim was lost ...may be made into a shroud for a corpse. R. Joseph observed: This implies that the commandments will be abolished in the Hereafter....for R. Johanan stated: 'What is the purport of the Scriptural text, 'Free among the dead'? As soon as a man dies he is free from the commandments'." (Nid.61b citing Ps. 88:5 [v.6 in English], cf.Shab.151b)

2. Hayim Donin, To Be A Jew, Basic Books, 1991, P.146

3. Tzitzit, the fringes, were to be put on the corners

of every four-cornered garment. When garments were no longer made with four corners, the Rabbis decreed that a special garment, the *tallit katan* [small tallis] or *arba kanfot* [four corners], be made and worn so that the commandment could still be fulfilled.

However, the blue dye used for the commanded blue thread came from a particular mollusc. For the last nineteen hundred years, that mollusc has been hard to find. The Rabbis decreed that no substitute blue could be used. They also decreed that the blue thread was not necessary. (Men.IV) So the contemporary *tallit* and *tallit katan* are made without the blue thread required by scripture.

SHABBAT

What is the purpose and meaning of Shabbat in the Covenant of the Law? There are four major reasons God gives for commanding Israel to keep the seventh day holy:

1. **A Memorial of Creation**
2. **A Memorial of Deliverance from Egypt**
3. **A Covenant Sign**
4. **A Time of Rest — A Tithe of Time**

1. A Memorial of Creation

The holiness of the seventh day, and its character as a day of rest, does not come from the Covenant of the Law. It does not come from the Ten Commandments. It does not come from Israel. It is what God decreed in creating this universe. It is part of God's revelation of Himself, and of the nature of man. God created the Sabbath.

"On the seventh day God finished His work which He had made; and He rested on the seventh day from all his work which He had made. And God blessed the seventh day and made it holy, because on it He rested from all the work of creating that he had done." (Gen. 2:2-3)

On the sixth day, "God created Adam in his own image, in the image of God He created him; male and female He created them....The LORD God took the man and put him in the Garden of Eden to work it and take care of it." (Gen. 1:27; 2:15) God created Adam and Eve on the sixth day. He rested on the seventh day, the day He made holy.

What did Adam and Eve, made in the image and likeness of God, do on the seventh day while God rested? Did they work, or did they rest? What did

God want them to do?

God did not create the Sabbath for Himself. He had no need to rest. As Yeshua said, "The Sabbath was made for Adam...." (Mark 2:27)

God created all of space and time. Out of all that He made, there was only one thing that He specifically made holy. God made the seventh day holy, specially set apart to Him.

God created Israel to be His witness, i.e. to testify of who He is. (e.g. Gen.43:10) He commanded Israel to commemorate His work of creation and His rest by observing the holiness of the seventh day.

"Remember the Sabbath day by keeping it holy. Six days you shall labor and do all your work, but the seventh day is a Sabbath to the LORD your God. On it you shall not do any work, neither you, nor your son or daughter, nor your manservant or maidservant, nor your animals, nor the alien within your gates. For in six days the LORD made the heavens and the earth, the sea, and all that is in them, but He rested on the seventh day. Therefore the LORD blessed the Sabbath day and made it holy." (Ex.20:8-11)

By observing the seventh day as a holy day of rest, all Israel was to bear witness that God is the creator and owner of all things. As it says in Psaalm 24:1, "The earth is the LORD's, and everything in it, the world, and all who live in it."

2. A Memorial of Deliverance from Egypt

For Israel, the Sabbath was to memorialize the deliverance from Egypt and the reward of freedom. We had been under cruel bondage, forced to work without rest, but God set us free.

"Observe the Sabbath day by keeping it holy, as

the LORD your God has commanded you. Six days you shall labor and do all your work, but the seventh day is a Sabbath to the LORD your God. On it you shall not do any work, neither you, nor your son or daughter, nor your manservant or maidservant, nor your ox, your donkey or any of your animals, nor the alien within your gates, so that your manservant and maidservant may rest, as you do.

"Remember that you were slaves in Egypt and that the LORD your God brought you out of there with a mighty hand and an outstretched arm. Therefore the LORD your God has commanded you to observe the Sabbath day." (Dt.5:12-15)

In addition to Shabbat being a celebration of freedom, it is also a reminder that we belong to the Lord. That is the reason for our freedom. "I am the LORD who brought you up out of Egypt to be your God; therefore be holy, because I am holy." (Lev. 11:45) God redeemed Israel to serve Him in holiness, i.e. as a people set apart for His purposes.

3. A Covenant Sign

The Sabbath itself is a covenant sign between God and Israel. God set apart the seventh day and sanctified it. He did the same with Israel.

"You must observe My Sabbaths. This will be a sign between Me and you for the generations to come, so you may know that I am the LORD, who makes you holy....The children of Israel are to observe the Sabbath, celebrating it for the generations to come as a lasting covenant. It will be a sign between Me and the children of Israel forever, for in six days the LORD made the heavens and the earth, and on the seventh day He abstained from work and rested." (Ex.31:13,16,17)

Israel's observance of Shabbat testifies that we are a people set apart to God, and not slaves to the world. Israel did not make itself holy. God made Israel holy. "Also I gave them My Sabbaths as a sign between us, so they would know that I the LORD made them holy." (Ezek. 20:12)

4. A Time of Rest — A Tithe of Time

God commanded that every one of the children of Israel bring to Him a tithe, a tenth, of what his labor produced. All of that labor belonged to the Lord, but He asked only for a tenth as a recognition of His sovereignty. That recognition would ensure the Lord's protection and blessing on the other nine-tenths.

In the same way, God commanded Israel to rest on the Sabbath. "Six days do your work, but on the seventh day do not work, so that your ox and your donkey may rest and the slave born in your household, and the alien as well, may be refreshed." (Ex. 23:12) Animals, servants, and strangers in the land were to have their rest as well.

In the wilderness, God showed that He would provide for His people on every day, including Shabbat. (cf.Ex.16:22-30) He wanted Israel to trust in His provision. Without faith in Him, there is no rest.

God commanded that even the land of Israel "must keep a sabbath to the Lord." (Lev. 25:2) In every seventh year, the land was to be allowed to rest. And after every seven sabbatical years, there was to be a year of jubilee, a year of restoration and liberation, for the land of Israel and for the people of Israel. (Lev. 25:8-12)

God warned of the judgment of exile among the nations for Israel's failure to let the land observe its sabbatical years. "Then the land will enjoy its sabbath years all the time that it lies desolate and you are in the country of your enemies; then the land will rest and enjoy its sabbaths. All the time that it lies desolate, the land will have the rest it did not have during the sabbaths you lived in it....For the land will be deserted by them and will enjoy its sabbaths while it lies desolate without them. They will pay for their sins because they rejected My laws and abhorred My decrees." (Lev. 26:34-35,43)

Breaking the Sabbath Brings Death

Keeping the Sabbath is one of the Ten Commandments, which God engraved in stone for Israel to show the way He wanted her to live. Keeping the Sabbath is engraved alongside "I am the Lord your God...You shall not murder....You shall not bear false witness." It is that important.

It is repeated in connection with these other great commandments. " 'Each of you must respect his mother and father, and you must observe my Sabbaths. I am the LORD your God. Do not turn to idols or make gods of cast metal for yourselves. I am the LORD your God." Lev. (19:3-4)

God considered the observance of the Sabbath so important for Israel that He commanded the community to put to death anyone who broke the Sabbath. "For six days, work is to be done, but the seventh day shall be your holy day, a Sabbath of rest to the LORD. Whoever does any work on it must be put to death." (Ex. 35:2)

"Observe the Sabbath, because it is holy to you. Anyone who desecrates it must be put to death; whoever does any work on that day must be cut off from his people.

95

"For six days, work is to be done, but the seventh day is a Sabbath of rest, holy to the LORD. Whoever does any work on the Sabbath day must be put to death." (Ex.31:14-15)

During the time in the wilderness, God was tested on this commandment. "While the children of Israel were in the desert, a man was found gathering wood on the Sabbath day. Those who found him gathering wood brought him to Moses and Aaron and the whole assembly, and they kept him in custody, because it was not clear what should be done to him.

"Then the LORD said to Moses, 'The man must die. The whole assembly must stone him outside the camp.' So the assembly took him outside the camp and stoned him to death, as the LORD commanded Moses." (Num. 15:32-36) God meant exactly what He said. The penalty for breaking the Sabbath was death.

National Punishment for Breaking the Sabbath

When God made Israel a holy nation, He gave her His special feasts to observe. The Sabbath is the first of these.

"These are My appointed feasts, the appointed feasts of the LORD, which you are to proclaim as sacred assemblies. There are six days when you may work, but the seventh day is a Sabbath of rest, a day of sacred assembly. You are not to do any work; wherever you live, it is a Sabbath to the LORD." (Lev. 23:2-3)

In Isaiah, God rebuked Israel for profaning the Sabbath and the other feasts of the Lord. "Stop bringing meaningless offerings! Your incense is detestable to me. New Moons, Sabbaths and convocations — I cannot bear your evil assemblies.

Your New Moon festivals and your appointed feasts My soul hates. They have become a burden to Me; I am weary of bearing them. When you spread out your hands in prayer, I will hide My eyes from you; even if you offer many prayers, I will not listen. Your hands are full of blood; wash and make yourselves clean. Take your evil deeds out of My sight! Stop doing wrong, learn to do right! Seek justice, encourage the oppressed. Defend the cause of the fatherless, plead the case of the widow." (Isa. 1:13)

God was not denouncing the Sabbath and the feasts which He instituted. Nor was He denouncing prayer. He was denouncing the way the people were perverting these things through their violence and unrighteousness. The inward corruption of the people, and the violent fruit which it produced, made any outward observance a detestable mockery.

Among Israel's other sins was the failure to observe God's Sabbath. In fact, the failure to keep the Sabbath was a major cause of God's denunciation and judgment. Ezekiel delivered many of God's rebukes to the people in exile.

"Yet the people of Israel rebelled against Me in the desert. They did not follow My decrees but rejected My laws —although the man who obeys them will live by them —and they utterly desecrated My Sabbaths. So I said I would pour out My wrath on them and destroy them in the desert. But for the sake of My name I did what would keep it from being profaned in the eyes of the nations in whose sight I had brought them out.

"Also with uplifted hand I swore to them in the desert that I would not bring them into the land I had given them —a land flowing with milk and honey, most beautiful of all lands — because they rejected My laws and did not follow My decrees and desecrated My Sabbaths. For their hearts were devoted to their idols.

"Keep My Sabbaths holy, that they may be a sign between us. Then you will know that I am the LORD your God. But the children rebelled against Me: They did not follow My decrees, they were not careful to keep My laws —although the man who obeys them will live by them —and they desecrated My Sabbaths. So I said I would pour out My wrath on them and spend My anger against them in the desert." (Ezek. 20:13-21)

God says "**My** Sabbaths." He punished Israel for desecrating **His** Sabbaths which He had given as a gracious gift.

The Blessings of Keeping the Sabbath

On the other hand, God promised great blessing if Israel would keep the Sabbath. "If you keep your feet from breaking the Sabbath and from doing as you please on My holy day, if you call the Sabbath a delight and the LORD's holy day honorable, and if you honor it by not going your own way and not doing as you please or speaking idle words, then you will find your joy in the LORD, and I will cause you to ride on the heights of the land and to feast on the inheritance of your father Jacob." (Isa. 58:13-14)

Keeping the Sabbath would even ensure the continuity of the Davidic kingdom. "If you are careful to obey Me, declares the LORD, and bring no load through the gates of this city on the Sabbath, but keep the Sabbath day holy by not doing any work on it, then kings who sit on David's throne will come through the gates of this city with their officials. They and their officials will come riding in chariots and

98

on horses, accompanied by the men of Judah and those living in Jerusalem, and this city will be inhabited forever.

"People will come from the towns of Judah and the villages around Jerusalem, from the territory of Benjamin and the western foothills, from the hill country and the Negev, bringing burnt offerings and sacrifices, grain offerings, incense and thank offerings to the house of the LORD. " (Jer. 17:24-26)

Observance in the Future

God makes it clear in Tanakh that the observance of the Sabbath will continue in the Messianic age. (e.g. Ezek. 45:17, 46:1-4) He also makes it clear that the observance of the Sabbath will continue in the ages to come, even in the time of the new heavens and earth. In that time, all the nations will join with Israel in celebrating Shabbat.

" 'As the new heavens and the new earth that I make will endure before Me,' declares the LORD, 'so will your name and descendants endure. From one New Moon to another and from one Sabbath to another, all mankind will come and bow down before Me,' says the LORD." (Is.66:22-23)

Gentiles and the Sabbath

There is no Biblical indication that God ever commanded the Gentiles to observe Shabbat. Throughout the Bible, Gentiles are condemned for transgressing different universal laws of God. They are condemned for transgressing each of the Ten Commandments, except for one — keeping the Sabbath.

Yet the Sabbath is the one feast of the Lord which Gentiles are specifically invited and encouraged to keep. God promises to bless **anyone** who keeps the Sabbath.

"This is what the LORD says: 'Maintain justice and do what is right, for My salvation is close at hand and My righteousness will soon be revealed. Blessed is the man who does this, the man who holds it fast, who keeps the Sabbath without desecrating it, and keeps his hand from doing any evil.

"Let no foreigner who has bound himself to the LORD say, 'The LORD will surely exclude me from His people.' And let not any eunuch complain, 'I am only a dry tree.' For this is what the LORD says: 'To the eunuchs who keep My Sabbaths, who choose what pleases Me and hold fast to My covenant — to them I will give within My temple and its walls a memorial and a name better than sons and daughters; I will give them an everlasting name that will not be cut off.

" 'And foreigners who bind themselves to the LORD to serve Him, to love the name of the LORD, and to worship Him, all who keep the Sabbath without desecrating it and who hold fast to My covenant — these I will bring to My holy mountain and give them joy in My house of prayer. Their burnt offerings and sacrifices will be accepted on My altar; for My house will be called a house of prayer for all nations.' " (Isa. 56:1-7)

Gentiles are not commanded to keep the Sabbath, but they are encouraged to do so. Those Gentiles who join themselves to the Lord and keep His Sabbaths will receive joy and an eternal inheritance from the Lord. God always intended Shabbat to be a blessing, not a burden.

Shabbat in the New Covenant

Now we can examine the place of Shabbat in the New Covenant. Despite the importance that God placed upon the Sabbath, and the blessings He promised for keeping it, we and our fathers did not keep it. Consequently, all the judgments He promised came upon us.

We did not obey God. We did not rest, and we did not let the land rest. So we were sent into exile. Then "The land enjoyed its sabbath rests; all the time of its desolation it rested, until the seventy years were completed in fulfillment of the word of the LORD spoken by Jeremiah." (2Chr. 36:21)

Even after the return from the Babylonian exile, we still did not keep the Sabbath. (e.g. Neh.13:15-22) God had redeemed us from slavery in Egypt and invited us, commanded us, to enter His rest, but we never did. We never submitted to the one who redeemed us. Our failure to keep the Sabbath was so complete that the Rabbis later said that if Israel were to keep one Sabbath, Messiah would come.

In an effort to protect the sanctity of the Sabbath, the Pharisees surrounded it with many laws. The Law of God had commanded the observance of Shabbat, but had not produced that observance. The Pharisees were mistaken in thinking that the laws of men could produce what the Law of God could not. They tried to compel obedience by restricting Israel's actions even more. They prohibited what God had approved.

It was into that atmosphere that Yeshua came, teaching that, "The Sabbath was made for man, not man for the Sabbath." (Mark 2:27) For him, the Sabbath was a time to teach, to heal, to set people free. The Pharisees did not see it that way.

"Indignant because Yeshua had healed on the

Sabbath, the synagogue ruler said to the people, 'There are six days for work. So come and be healed on those days, not on the Sabbath.'

"The Lord answered him, 'You hypocrites! Doesn't each of you on the Sabbath untie his ox or donkey from the stall and lead it out to give it water? Then should not this woman, a daughter of Abraham, whom Satan has kept bound for eighteen long years, be set free on the Sabbath day from what bound her?' " (Luke 13:14-16)

God had commanded that even the animals should rest on Shabbat. For that to take place, it was necessary that the animals be given water and fed. Cows needed to be milked, or they would be in great pain. In the sight of God, there was a difference between doing those chores so that the animals could rest and doing the same chores for the owner's economic benefit. The same act was both permitted and prohibited, depending upon the motivation. The same act was both commanded and prohibited.

It was also recognized that circumcision — i.e. initiating a child into the Abrahamic covenant — took precedence over Shabbat. So did saving a life. So did the Passover. (cf. Pesachim 65b-66a)

Accordingly, consistent with Torah, Yeshua taught, "How much more valuable is a man than a sheep! Therefore it is lawful to do good on the Sabbath." (Mt. 12:12) God is the definer of what is good. Yeshua was not teaching men to break the law, for it is holy, righteous, and good, He was teaching them how to uphold it.

The following generations of Rabbis added still more laws. In the words of the Talmud, "The laws concerning the Sabbath... are as mountains hanging by a hair, for they have scant scriptural basis but many laws." (Hag.10a) These laws were the creation of the Rabbis, but the Sabbath is a time to celebrate God setting us free from the slavery of men.

The Rabbis had it backwards when they said that if Israel were to keep one Sabbath, Messiah would come. It is the coming of Messiah that enables us to keep the Sabbath. When he comes, he brings the New Covenant. Through the New Covenant we receive the Spirit of the Lord to enable us to walk in obedience.

"There remains, then, a Sabbath-rest for the people of God; for anyone who enters God's rest also rests from his own work, just as God did from His." (Hebr. 4:9-10)

Keeping the Sabbath

We all need rest for our souls, but we usually live according to the demands of our schedules. If we can rest, we do. If we can't, we don't. We know that God could rest, but we can't, because we have so much to do.

We forget what Solomon in all his wisdom learned: "Unless the LORD builds the house, its builders labor in vain. Unless the LORD watches over the city, the watchmen stand guard in vain. In vain you rise early and stay up late, toiling for food to eat — for He grants sleep to those He loves." (Ps. 127:1-2)

There is something displeasing to God in our unceasing labor. As David said in Psalm 23:2, "He makes me lie down in green pastures. He leads me to waters of rest."

Yeshua proclaimed that the Sabbath was made for man. In Hebrew, his words are more revealing: "Shabbat was made for Adam, not Adam for

Shabbat." God created Adam on the sixth day. He made the seventh day a day of rest for Adam's sake. God Himself had no need to rest. If we, the descendants of Adam, do not rest, we distort the nature and purpose of our own lives.

We must first accept the fact that the Lord is in charge of building the house. It is the Lord who gives us rest. It is the Lord who makes us holy.

Shabbat was made for us, but that doesn't mean that we can do with it as we please. All things are to be used according to the purpose for which God created them. In doing that, we receive from these created things what the Creator intends for us to receive.

The Sabbath is a time to humbly commemorate the creation of God, and recognize our need for His deliverance. It is a time to cease from the business — religious and otherwise — of men. When we enter into the rest of God, then we can keep the Sabbath. God tells us that we keep the Sabbath holy, "If you keep...from doing as you please..., if you honor it by not going your own way and not doing as you please or speaking idle words." (Isa. 58:13-14)

God's purpose for Shabbat remains the same. That is why we are told, "There remains, then, a Sabbath-rest for the people of God; for anyone who enters God's rest also rests from his own work, just as God did from His. Let us, therefore, make every effort to enter that rest, so that no one will fall by following their example of disobedience." (Hebr. 4:9-11)

Observance of the holy Sabbath flows from a relationship with the Holy One. When we seek to minutely specify what is permitted and what is prohibited, we substitute law for relationship. **THE** law of Shabbat is, "Do not do your own will. Do what

God wants you to do."

Can people be mistaken, confused, or deceived about what God wants them to do? Of course. However, the path to clarity is not human legislation, but rather developing a closer relationship with God. It is not in the decrees of an elite. It is in taking individual responsibility for one's own life before God, and walking humbly with God. For God characterizes the New Covenant as one in which "you shall all know Me, from the least of them to the greatest of them." (Jer.31:34)

By resting from labor, Israel was to proclaim that the earth belongs to the Lord, Israel belongs to the Lord, and all her work belongs to the Lord. All things, especially His people, belong to Him. All the work that is done on the other six days must be done in the light of that. We were slaves of men, but God set us free. We are to live, work, and rest as free men, not as slaves of other people or things.

All that we have belongs to God, but we follow the faith and example of Abraham (and Jacob) in giving a tithe to God. The tithe is not a substitute for godly living. It should be its fruit, a tangible recognition of the sovereignty of God. Yeshua warned, "Woe to you, teachers of the law and Pharisees, you hypocrites! You give a tenth of your spices —mint, dill and cummin. But you have neglected the more important matters of the law — justice, mercy and faithfulness. You should have practiced the latter, without neglecting the former." (Matt. 23:23)

In the same way, all our time belongs to God, but setting apart Shabbat is like a tithe, a tangible recognition of His sovereignty over time. It is not a substitute for, nor the measure of, a godly life. It should be its fruit.

In every week there is a seventh day.[1] In fact, it is the seventh day that divides time and makes a week a week. The seventh day is the end of the week. The seventh day is Shabbat. God made it so when He created the world. It will still be so when He creates the new heavens and the new earth. God rested on the seventh day and made it holy. That is forever true.

We can choose to live as though we were not set apart to God, and we can choose to live as though the seventh day were not set apart to God, but God has called us to live as a holy people. He made us holy, saying to our fathers, "I am the LORD, who makes you holy....The children of Israel are to observe the Sabbath, celebrating it for the generations to come as an everlasting covenant." (Ex.31:13,16)

FOOTNOTE
1. Some theologians have taught that Sunday has become Shabbat. There is not a single scripture anywhere in the Bible that says anything even remotely supportive of such a teaching.

Reference is sometimes made to 1 Corinthians 16:1-2, but these verses say nothing about such a change. Nor do they even mention congregational meetings on Sunday.

The argument is made that Sunday is "the Lord's day," the day on which Yeshua rose from the dead, citing Revelation 1:9-10. It would seem most consistent to understand the phrase used there in the same way that we read throughout the Scriptures of "the day of the Lord," a time when God brings judgment on the earth.

This is exactly what John then describes in

Revelation. He makes no mention of the Sabbath. Nor does he make any connection between "the Lord's day" and Yeshua's resurrection. The visions of God's coming judgments are given to him when he is alone in exile on the Isle of Patmos. There is no mention of congregational meetings or anything which has come to be associated with Sunday. The equation of "the Lord's day" with Sunday took place centuries later.

Beyond all this, the first day is the first day, not the seventh. God created Shabbat as the commemoration of the **conclusion** of His work of creation. The first day cannot do that.

Sunday is a fine day for meeting, worshipping God, resting, or commemorating the resurrection of Messiah, but it is not the seventh day. The seventh day is the one which God made holy. Shabbat commemorates the completion of God's creative work.

DIFFICULT PASSAGES

There are passages in the New Covenant writings that are often assumed to teach the annulment of the law of God. Sometimes this is because of mistranslation, sometimes it is because of misinterpretation. The confusion surrounds four major issues: **clean and unclean foods, the means of being justified before God, the differences between Jews and Gentiles, and the continued applicability of the Law of Moses.**

Clean and Unclean Foods

The distinction between clean and unclean animals is not first presented in the Covenant of the Law. God told Noah, "Take with you seven of every kind of clean animal, a male and its mate, and two of every kind of unclean animal, a male and its mate." (Gen7:2) Noah was expected to know which animals were clean and which were unclean. At that time, God had not yet given man permission to eat animals. (cf. Gen.1:29; 9:3) The distinction was one God had already made long before Abraham, and long before Sinai.

After the flood, God permitted man to eat meat. The Covenant of the Law did not establish which animals were clean and which were unclean. It merely commanded Israel not to eat the flesh of unclean animals.

a) In **Mark 7:14-19**, Yeshua speaks of how our unclean words defile us. Some translations have significantly changed the text so that it becomes a very troublesome passage.

Here is a fairly literally presentation of the text. The King James Version, Phillips, and the New

English Bible present essentially the same.

"Again Yeshua called the crowd and said to them, 'Listen to me, everyone, and understand. There is nothing outside a man that can defile him by going into him, but the things which go out from him, those are the things which defile the man. If anyone has ears to hear, let him hear.'

"And when he left the crowd and went into a house, his disciples asked him about this parable. And he said to them, 'Are you also without understanding? Don't you perceive that nothing that enters a man from the outside can defile him? Because it doesn't go into his heart but into his stomach, and is eliminated, purifying all the food.'"

The problem does not arise from the text itself. The problem arises from some interpretative translations of the text. In understanding this text, some translators have chosen to neglect the text and follow Origen, a heretic who maintained that the Bible had to be allegorized to be understood, and John Chrysostom, a violent anti-semite.

Here is the New International Version of the last two verses " 'Don't you see that nothing that enters a man from the outside can make him unclean? For it doesn't go into his heart but into his stomach, and then out of his body.' (In saying this, Jesus declared all foods clean.)" (Mark 7:18-19) Others — NASV, RSV, LB, TEV, Jerusalem Bible — have similar translations.

The parenthetical comment was created by inserting "In saying this, Jesus declared" into the text. These words are actually not in the Bible. Then the translators changed the verb "purifying" to the adjective "clean", and dropped the definite article "the". The resulting translation turns the text into a doctrinal pronouncement on clean and unclean animals. There is no basis for it in the text. It is unrelated to thelanguage and the context.

The word translated as "food" is a generic word referring to food of any kind — fruit, vegetables, grains, meats, etc. Yeshua was speaking of the natural biological process that takes place when a person eats any food. He was not defining what qualifies as food.

God had already done that. God had given to Adam every seed-bearing plant and every seed-bearing fruit of a tree. (Gen. 1:29) After the flood, God also gave to all the descendants of Noah every moving creature as food. (Gen. 9:3) At Sinai, God declared some moving creatures, the unclean ones, to no longer be food for the children of Israel. (Lev.11) God commanded, "You must distinguish between the unclean and the clean, between living creatures that may be eaten and those that may not be eaten." (Lev. 11:47) Some things are food, some things are not. God is the One who determines what goes into which category.

What Yeshua said was a direct response to the accusation of some Pharisees that his disciples were eating with hands that were not washed according to the traditions of the elders. (Mk.7:1-5) He was addressing the hypocrisy of being clean on the outside, but unclean on the inside. (cf. Mt.23:25-26)

b) In **Gal. 2:11-14**, Paul speaks of Peter's vacillation and hypocrisy in first eating with the Gentiles and then not eating with them. So some have assumed that Peter was eating what was prohibited to Jews by Torah. The text does not say that. **The issue is not WHAT Peter ate, but WITH WHOM he ate.**

"When Peter came to Antioch, I opposed him to

110

his face, because he was clearly in the wrong. Before certain men came from Jacob, he used to eat with the Gentiles. But when they arrived, he began to draw back and separate himself from the Gentiles because he was afraid of those who belonged to the circumcision group.

"The other Jews joined him in his hypocrisy, so that by their hypocrisy even Barnabas was led astray. When I saw that they were not acting in line with the truth of the gospel, I said to Peter in front of them all, 'You are a Jew, yet you live like a Gentile and not like a Jew. How is it, then, that you force Gentiles to live as Jews?' "

Peter had been eating with the uncircumcised Gentile believers, indicating that God had cleansed them through the atonement of Yeshua. Some Jews from Jerusalem came and were teaching that these Gentiles needed to be circumcised before they could be truly admitted into the community of Israel and therefore before Jews could eat with them.

Peter knew that was not true, but out of fear he stopped eating with the Gentiles. Paul condemned Peter's hypocrisy.

The question that Paul addresses throughout Galatians is that of justification, i.e. how a person can be righteous before God. His answer is that all people, whether Jewish or Gentile, can be righteous before God in the same way that God declared Abraham to be, by faith. (cf. Gen.15:6) Abraham was not circumcised at that time.

Peter knew these things, and had been living according to them in eating with the Gentile believers. He was fellowshipping with the uncircumcised believers, thereby testifying that they did not need to be circumcised and live according to the Law of

Moses in order to be justified before God. When he withdrew from them in his hypocrisy, he was acting as if all men needed to become Jews to be justified. That is the point of Paul's question: "How is it, then, that you force Gentiles to live as Jews?"

This was not a discussion of what Peter or the Gentiles were eating. That is not mentioned. Peter had separated himself from the Gentiles because they were uncircumcised. In doing that, he was falsely testifying that Gentiles needed to be circumcised before they could be admitted to fellowship in Israel. Peter was forcing the Gentiles to live as Jews.

In what way was Peter himself living like a Gentile? Paul described how Gentiles lived, "in every kind of impurity, with a continual lust for more." (Eph. 4:17) They lived in lustful passion, denying God. (1Ths. 4:5) They lived in rebellion against their Creator and their own created nature. (Rom.1:18-32)

Is that how Peter was living? No. Peter himself cautioned against living as the Gentiles did, "in debauchery, lust, drunkenness, orgies, carousing and detestable idolatry." (1Pet. 4:3) In what way then was Peter living as a Gentile?

The men who had come were saying that Jews should not have table fellowship with Gentile believers who were uncircumcised. In effect, they were saying, "Jews do not eat with uncircumcised Gentiles. Any Jew who does is not really a Jew." As Peter said to Cornelius, "You are well aware that it is against our law for a Jew to associate with a Gentile or visit him." (Acts 10:28)

There is a parallel to this in the Talmud. "R. Nahman b. Isaac said to the people, 'Cut off all relationship with Aibu because he eats the bread of Gentiles.' " (Avodah Zarah 35b) It is not the bread itself that is unclean. It is its relationship to the Gentiles, i.e. the uncircumcised, that makes it unclean. Anyone who is eating their bread should be treated as though he were one of them.

"He who eats the bread of a Cuthean [a disguised reference to "Gentiles"] is as one who eats the flesh of swine." (Chullin 13a, Soncino CD n.23 in reference to V.Sheb.VIII,10) Eating the bread of Gentiles makes a person like the Gentiles. In this view, there can be no fellowship with uncircumcised Gentiles, or with any Jew who has table fellowship with Gentiles.

There is also a parallel in the writings of Paul. "But now I am writing you that you must not associate with anyone who calls himself a brother but is sexually immoral or greedy, an idolater or a slanderer, a drunkard or a swindler. With such a man do not even eat." (1 Co.5:11) Eating with such a man would be a declaration that the man is clean.

c. Acts 10:13-15 Before God sent Peter to speak to the Roman centurion Cornelius, He showed him a vision of every kind of animal and reptile. When he saw the vision, Peter did not understand what it meant. (v.17) At Cornelius' house, Peter understood and explained what the vision meant. (v.28)

Acts 10:13-15,17: "Then a voice told him, 'Get up, Peter. Kill and eat.'

" 'Surely not, Lord!' Peter replied. 'I have never eaten anything impure or unclean.'

"The voice spoke to him a second time, 'Do not call anything impure that God has made clean.' ...

"While Peter was wondering about the meaning of the vision, the men sent by Cornelius found out where Simon's house was and stopped at the gate."

At that time, Peter did not know what the vision

meant. He had walked with Yeshua from the beginning of his ministry, but had never understood anything Yeshua said to indicate that all animals were clean and therefore to be considered as food. [The gospel of Mark is said to be written from the information Peter supplied.]

After God poured out His Spirit on Cornelius and those with him, Peter understood the meaning of the vision. As he said to Cornelius, "You are well aware that it is against our law for a Jew to associate with a Gentile or visit him. **But God has shown me that I should not call any man impure or unclean."** (v.28)

Peter understood the vision to mean that God could make Gentiles clean. That is how he later explained it when his actions were questioned.

"So when Peter went up to Jerusalem, the circumcised believers criticized him and said, 'You went into the house of uncircumcised men and ate with them.' " (Acts 11:2-3)

He explained to them the vision of the animals and how God had poured out His Holy Spirit on Cornelius and his household. " 'So if God gave them the same gift as He gave us, who believed in the Lord Yeshua the Messiah, who was I to think that I could oppose God?'

"When they heard this, they had no further objections and praised God, saying, 'So then, God has granted even the Gentiles repentance unto life.' " (Acts 11:17-18)

When the other Jewish believers understood that God had cleansed the Gentiles, "they had no further objection." No one mentioned **what** Peter ate when he was in the house of Cornelius. The issue was **with whom** he ate.

During the Council that was called to determine

the relationship of the Gentiles to the Law of Moses, Peter again related what took place at the house of Cornelius. "God, who knows the heart, showed that he accepted them by giving the Holy Spirit to them, just as he did to us. He made no distinction between us and them, for he purified their hearts by faith." (Acts 15:8-9) People who had been considered unclean were cleansed.

No one, including Peter, understood the vision or incident to mean that Jews should no longer observe the God-given distinction between clean and unclean animals. No one even mentions such a thought. That distinction was one that God had made in the days of Noah. (cf. Gen.7:2)

According to Jacob, all the Jewish believers were zealous for the Law of Moses. (Acts 21:20) According to the historical record, all the apostles, including Peter and Paul, scrupulously lived according to the Law of Moses. There is no evidence to the contrary.

d) In **1Tim. 4:1-5**, Paul speaks of false teaching that prohibits the eating of certain foods. Doesn't this show that all animals are permitted as food for all people?

"The Spirit clearly says that in later times some will abandon the faith and follow deceiving spirits and things taught by demons. Such teachings come through hypocritical liars, whose consciences have been seared as with a hot iron. They forbid people to marry and order them to abstain from certain foods which God created to be received with thanksgiving by those who believe and who know the truth.

"For everything God created is good, and nothing is to be rejected if it is received with thanksgiving, because it is consecrated by the word of God and prayer."

God gave the Torah to Israel and prohibited specific types of marriage, i.e. the marriage of certain close relatives. When Paul wrote to Timothy, no one was teaching that incest was now permissible. That wasn't the issue. But some were teaching, or would in the future teach, that marriages which God had permitted were now prohibited.

Some would teach that certain people were forbidden to marry. Paul refers to this elsewhere. "This is my defense to those who sit in judgment on me.... Don't we have the right to take a believing wife along with us, as do the other apostles and the Lord's brothers and Cephas?" (1Cor. 9:3,5)

The same thing was true of food. God had specified what things were "foods" to be received with thanksgiving and what things were not. Blood is not a food, though some people eat it. Human beings are not food, though some people eat human flesh.

There were those who were teaching, or would teach, that it was wrong to eat certain foods which God had permitted. They were prohibiting what God had permitted. Paul was not talking about God's prohibitions. He was talking about demonically inspired teaching that forbids marriage which God has permitted and forbids foods which God has permitted.

e) Col. 2:16-17,20-22: "Therefore do not let anyone judge you by what you eat or drink, or with regard to a religious festival, a New Moon celebration or a Sabbath day. These are a shadow of the things that were to come; the reality, however, is found in Messiah....

116

"Since you died with Messiah to the basic principles of this world, why, as though you still belonged to it, do you submit to its rules: 'Do not handle! Do not taste! Do not touch!'? These are all destined to perish with use, because they are based on human commands and teachings."

Paul says that laws concerning food and drink are just shadows. Does that mean they have passed away? What Paul says here, as with all his writings, must be understood in their context.

He is speaking as the Jewish apostle to the uncircumcised, i.e. Gentiles. In Col. 2:13, he makes it clear that he is speaking here to Gentiles. "When you were dead in your sins and **in the uncircumcision of your flesh**, God made you alive with Messiah....."

The laws relating to clean and unclean animals, the Feasts of the Lord, the New Moon celebration and the Sabbath were given to Israel in the Covenant of the Law. Gentile believers do not have their relationship with God through the Covenant of the Law. They have their relationship with God through His New Covenant with Israel. Therefore, Gentile believers are not expected to keep the specific laws given to Israel

Paul does not say, "Do these things," or "Do not do these things." He simply says, "Do not let anyone judge you in terms of these things, whether you do them or not."

What does Paul mean when he says that these things are a shadow of what is to come? He means that they are symbolic of a greater reality. Human marriage is a type of the marriage of the Lord to His people. Human fatherhood is a type of divine fatherhood. Life is a shadow of the life to come. That does not mean that we should do away with all these things.

The fact that there is a greater reality does not mean that the shadow or type has no significance and should be discarded. On the contrary, the shadows and types are given for a purpose, and help us to understand the greater reality. They give us visible content. They are simply not an end in themselves. They point to what is to come. In this case, that is Messiah.

In the following verse, Paul says, "Do not let anyone who delights in false humility and the worship of angels disqualify you for the prize. Such a person goes into great detail about what he has seen, and his unspiritual mind puffs him up with idle notions." (Col. 2:18) There were people who claimed to have special revelations from God, possibly through angels. They were judging and defrauding others on the basis of their personal revelations.

That is why it is generally believed that Paul was addressing problems in Colossae caused by gnostic teaching. That is why Paul says that, "Do not handle! Do not taste! Do not touch!'... are based on human commands and teachings." He was not talking about God's commandments, but about the decrees of certain self-proclaimed mystics.

As Paul wrote to Timothy, the Law, the Writings, and the Prophets were breathed by God. (2Tim.3:14-17) They were written as the human authors yielded to God's Spirit. They reveal the eternal character of God.

f) In **1Cor. 6:12-13**, doesn't Paul declare all foods clean?

" 'Everything is permissible for me'—but not everything is beneficial. 'Everything is permissible for me'—but I will not be mastered by anything. Food for the stomach and the stomach for food —but God will destroy them both. The body is not meant for sexual immorality, but for the Lord, and the Lord for the body."

Does Paul mean that he is free to do anything he chooses to, even if God had previously commanded him not to? No, that cannot be what he means, because he says that sexual immorality is not permitted. Just prior to this verse, he listed certain kinds of behavior that will keep a person out of the kingdom of God.

"Do you not know that the wicked will not inherit the kingdom of God? Do not be deceived: Neither the sexually immoral nor idolaters nor adulterers nor male prostitutes nor homosexuals, nor thieves nor the greedy nor drunkards nor slanderers nor swindlers will inherit the kingdom of God." (1Cor. 6:9-10)

These things are not permitted. Paul explicitly warned the Corinthians to have nothing to do with anyone who claimed a freedom to do these things: "But now I am writing you that you must not associate with anyone who calls himself a brother but is sexually immoral or greedy, an idolater or a slanderer, a drunkard or a swindler. With such a man do not even eat." (1Cor. 5:11)

What then does Paul mean in 1Cor.6:12-13? Paul's letters were written to deal with specific issues which had arisen in the different congregations. Paul knew that the believers in Corinth were quarreling about certain issues. (cf.1Cor. 1:11; 3:3)

It is generally understood that in responding to these quarrels, Paul sometimes first states the position that some have taken, and then responds. (cf.1Cor.

1:12; 3:4) That is why the translators of the NIV put 'Everything is permissible for me' in quotes to signify that this is what some of the Corinthian believers were saying. The phrase is then followed by Paul's responses: "but not everything is beneficial. ...but I will not be mastered by anything."

There was great sin in Corinth, and some were even boasting in it. (cf 1Co.5:1-6) "It is actually reported that there is sexual immorality among you, and of a kind that does not occur even among the Gentiles..." (1Cor. 5:1) Some of the Corinthian believers claimed that since Yeshua had died for their sins, they were free to do anything. Atonement had already been made for their sin. They were indulging themselves and ignoring the love and the life that is to characterize all followers of Yeshua.

Paul unequivocally, repeatedly rebuked them for doing this. The body is not meant to be indulged and used immorally. Loving God does not permit that. Loving one's neighbor does not permit that. Loving God and loving one's neighbor means that we submit our bodies to the righteousness defined by God. (cf. Rom.6:12-18)

g) In **1Cor. 8:8-9**, doesn't Paul say that it doesn't matter what we eat or don't eat?

"But food does not bring us near to God; we are no worse if we do not eat, and no better if we do. Be careful, however, that the exercise of your freedom does not become a stumbling block to the weak."

Paul told the Gentile believers in Corinth not to eat food sacrificed to idols. He explained that it is not the food itself that defiles or commends a person to God. It is our love of God and love of our neighbor that God is seeking.

Loving God requires that we obey Him. Part of obeying Him is loving our neighbor. "If anyone says, 'I love God,' yet hates his brother, he is a liar. For anyone who does not love his brother, whom he has seen, cannot love God, whom he has not seen." (1John 4:20)

To love God, we need to consider other people and faithfully show to them the Truth of God. That is why the Corinthians should not eat food sacrificed to idols. It does matter. "Let us not love with words or tongue but with actions and in truth." (1John 3:18)

Paul himself was very conscious of the effect of his own life on those he taught. He was very conscious of his calling to bring the Gentiles to obedience. That is why he said, "I will not venture to speak of anything except what Messiah has accomplished through me in leading the Gentiles to obey God by what I have said and done." (Rom. 15:18)

Paul told the Corinthians, "Circumcision is nothing and uncircumcision is nothing. Keeping God's commandments is what counts." (1Cor. 7:19) That enables us to better understand what he is saying here: "Food is nothing and refraining from eating food is nothing. Keeping God's commandments is what counts."

God commanded Israel not to eat certain animals. He said, "they are unclean for you." (e.g.Dt.14:7,10,19)

The Means of Being Justified before God
a) Gal. 2:15-21 "We who are Jews by birth and not 'Gentile sinners' know that a man is not justified by observing the law, but by faith in Yeshua the Messiah. So we, too, have put our faith in Messiah

Yeshua that we may be justified by faith in Messiah and not by observing the law, because by observing the law no one will be justified.

"If, while we seek to be justified in Messiah, it becomes evident that we ourselves are sinners, does that mean that Messiah promotes sin? Absolutely not! If I rebuild what I destroyed, I prove that I am a lawbreaker.

"For through the law I died to the law so that I might live for God. I have been crucified with Messiah and I no longer live, but Messiah lives in me. The life I live in the body, I live by faith in the Son of God, who loved me and gave himself for me. I do not set aside the grace of God, for if righteousness could be gained through the law, Messiah died for nothing!"

If a man murders his neighbor and is captured, a court will determine whether he is innocent or guilty. If the evidence shows his guilt, the court will find him guilty. The fact that there are hundreds and possibly thousands of other laws which he did not break does not remove his guilt for what he did that was wrong. The fact that he didn't rape anyone does not make him not guilty of murder.

If the murderer stands before God, he will find much the same thing. The murderer is guilty of breaking God's law. The fact that he didn't break other laws does not alter the fact that he is guilty of murder. The fact that he loves his mother does not make him not guilty.

The Bible teaches, and human experience confirms, that Solomon was right when he said, "there is no one who does not sin." (1Kgs. 8:46) No matter how many of God's laws we do keep, we do not always keep them all. Judged according to His law, we are all guilty before Him. Our actions do not make us righteous.

How then can a man be righteous before God? Long before the Law was given at Sinai, God showed the way.

Because of the evil of men's hearts, God determined, " 'I will wipe mankind, whom I have created, from the face of the earth —men and animals, and creatures that move along the ground, and birds of the air —for I am grieved that I have made them.' But Noah found grace in the eyes of the LORD." (Gen.6:7-8) Noah was righteous in his generation (v.9), but that was not sufficient. He still needed the grace of God.

He received the grace of God by believing God. His faith became evident to all. "By faith Noah, when warned about things not yet seen, in holy fear built an ark to save his family. By his faith he condemned the world and became heir of the righteousness that comes by faith." (Hebr. 11:7) By grace, he was saved through faith, to do the work that God set before him. (cf.Eph.2:8-10)

It was the same for Abraham. God was gracious to him. In response, "Abram believed the LORD, and He credited it to him as righteousness." (Gen. 15:6) Because of Abraham's faith in God, he obeyed and offered up Isaac.

God said to him, "...because you have done this and have not withheld your son, your only son, I will surely bless you and make your descendants as numerous as the stars in the sky and as the sand on the seashore. Your descendants will take possession of the cities of their enemies, and through your offspring all nations on earth will be blessed, because you have obeyed Me." (Gen. 22:16-18)

Yeshua willingly took upon himself the judgment of death which the law of God decrees for our sins. If we place our faith in him as the atonement which God provided, then God also counts our faith as righteousness. If we place our faith in him, then in his death we die to our own lives and to sin.

But to what is Paul referring when he says, "If I rebuild what I destroyed, I prove that I am a lawbreaker"? In general, the act of rebuilding shows that the destruction should not have taken place. Therefore, the act of rebuilding shows that the one who destroyed what must be rebuilt was in the wrong.

In this specific case, there is a closer reference at hand. Before God sent Peter to Cornelius, Peter had never eaten with Gentiles. There was a dividing wall between him and them.

By obeying God and going to Cornelius, Peter had entered into Messiah's work of tearing down that dividing wall between believing Jews and believing Gentiles. By withdrawing from the Gentiles, Peter was rebuilding what he had once destroyed. In doing that, he was testifying that he had transgressed before in tearing down the wall, i.e. in eating with the Gentiles. By withdrawing from the Gentiles, he was testifying against himself.

b) Gal. 3:10-11 "All who rely on observing the law are under a curse, for it is written: 'Cursed is everyone who does not continue to do everything written in the Book of the Law.' Clearly no one is justified before God by the law, because, 'The righteous will live by faith.' The law is not based on faith; on the contrary, 'The man who does these things will live by them.' "

If we seek to be righteous before God by our observance of the law, we will be disappointed. All the good we might do cannot atone for the times we break God's law. Before entering into the land, all Israel proclaimed a curse on everyone who breaks God's law.

We must find another way to be justified before God. That way is faith, the same means by which Abraham was considered righteous, the same means by which the Lord said that all the righteous should live. (Hab.2:4) The faith of Abraham is evidenced in our lives by our trusting and obeying God.

The differences between Jews and Gentiles

All of the scriptures in this section deal with very much the same issue. I have not repeated every explanation in each discussion. Therefore I would encourage you to read all the discussions to get a more complete picture.

a) Does **Eph. 2:14-16** teach that the Law is abolished and that Jews and Gentiles are now the same?

A literal translation of the text would be, "For he is our peace, who made both one and broke down the middle wall of the fence, **having annulled in his flesh the enmity of the law** of commandments in decrees, that he might create in himself the two into one new man, making peace; and might reconcile both in one body to God through the cross, **having slain the enmity by it.**"

The NIV translation reads: "For he himself is our peace, who has made the two one and has destroyed the barrier, the dividing wall of hostility, **by abolishing in his flesh the law** with its commandments and regulations. His purpose was to create in himself one new man out of the two, thus making peace, and in this one body to reconcile both of them to God through the cross, by which **he put to death their hostility.** "

The text itself does not say that the law is abolished. It is the enmity between Jew and Gentile, required by the law to keep Israel holy, that is annulled for believers. It is that enmity, the "middle wall" or "barrier," that is broken down. It is that enmity which was "slain" or "put to death."

The law of God which He gave to Israel contained decrees which separated the Jewish people from the Gentiles. This was in accordance with God's purpose of making Israel a holy nation. Because the Gentiles had rejected God and turned to idolatry and immorality, God commanded Israel to be a people set apart, living in light of the promises and covenants of God.

Messiah died for the sins of all. Gentiles who repent and believe in him are brought into the commonwealth of Israel through the New Covenant, so that they can share in the promises of God. (cf.Eph.2:12,19)

Towards these Gentile believers, the decrees in which God commanded Israel to be separate from the Gentiles have no work to do (*katargesa*). The purpose of the decrees was to keep Israel holy. (e.g. Ex.34:12-16) The Gentile believers have chosen to embrace a holy life, and are therefore incorporated into Israel. Being one with them does not make Jews unholy. They are made one with the believing Jewish remnant.

Ruth had made the same choice many centuries before. So had Rahab. They were brought into Israel. By God's design and purpose, King David, all the kings of Judah, and Messiah himself are descended from both Ruth and Rahab.

As for the separation, Paul makes the application to Gentile believers quite explicit. "Do not be yoked together with unbelievers. For what do righteousness and wickedness have in common? Or what fellowship can light have with darkness?" (2Cor. 6:14)

As for the two being made one, they are likened to one body. Paul clearly explained that different members of the same body have different appearances and functions. They are not supposed to be identical. They are supposed to be different. (1Cor. 12:17-20)

Adam and Eve were created separately and differently, so that they could become one. The differences are necessary for the two to become one. If the two were identical, they could not become one. The differences are part of God's design for mutual blessing, fruitfulness, and fulfillment.

b) In **Col. 2:13-14**, doesn't Paul say that the Law is put to death?

A literal translation of these verses would be: "When you were dead in your sins and in the uncircumcision of your flesh, God made you alive with Messiah. He forgave us all our sins, having blotted out the handwriting in the decrees against us, which was adversarial to us; He took it out of the midst, nailing it to the cross."

Paul, the Jewish apostle to the Gentiles, is writing to Gentiles who have become believers. He reminds them that "you were dead in your sins and in the uncircumcision of your flesh." Because of their sins, by the standard of God's universal law, a law which was revealed in them, they were judged guilty and sentenced to death.

That sentence was executed, not against them, but against Yeshua. No decree against them remains. As David said, "Blessed are they whose transgressions are forgiven, whose sins are covered. Blessed is the man whose sin the Lord will never count against him, and in whose spirit is no deceit." (Ps.32:1-2; Rom.4:7-8)

That is true for both Paul, a Jew, and the Gentile believers in Colosse to whom he is writing. But the Covenant of the Law contains decrees which separate Jews from Gentiles, as discussed above concerning Eph.2:14-16. These decrees stand in the middle, as a wall, between Jews and Gentiles.

Messiah, by dying for the sins of Gentiles as well as those of Jews, makes a way for the two to be one in him. The purpose of the decrees was to keep Israel from being polluted by the idolatry and immorality practiced by the Gentiles. They are not applicable to Gentiles who have been sanctified through Messiah's death. They do not divide believing Jews from believing Gentiles. They have been taken out of our midst.

c) **Gal. 3:28** "There is neither Jew nor Greek, slave nor free, male nor female, for you are all one in Messiah Yeshua." (cf. Col. 3:9)

Messiah is one, and everyone who believes in him is a member of his body. Each believer has access to God in the same way, through his death and his life. We are all the same in this.

Concerning our functions and callings, there are differences, because God did not make us identical. That is why Paul often separately addresses the very groups that have become one in Messiah — Jews (e.g.

Rom.7:1) and Gentiles (e.g. Rom. 15:25-27), slaves (e.g. Eph. 6:5) and masters (e.g. Eph. 6:9), men (e.g. Eph.5:25) and women (e.g. Eph. 5:22).

As he explains in 1Cor. 12:12,17-20: "For even as the body is one, though it is made up of many members; and though all the members of the body are many, they form one body. So it is with Messiah.... If the whole body were an eye, where would the sense of hearing be? If the whole body were an ear, where would the sense of smell be? But in fact God has arranged the parts in the body, every one of them, just as He wanted them to be. If they were all one part, where would the body be? As it is, there are many parts, but one body."

d) 1Cor. 7:18-20 "Was a man already circumcised when he was called? He should not become uncircumcised. Was a man uncircumcised when he was called? He should not be circumcised. Circumcision is nothing and uncircumcision is nothing. **Keeping God's commandments is what counts.** Each one should remain in the calling which he was in when God called him."

Those who are called as Jews should live as godly Jews. Those who are called as Gentiles should live as godly Gentiles. Each person should keep the commandments which God has given to him.

1Cor. 9:19-22 "Though I am free and belong to no man, I make myself a slave to everyone, to win as many as possible. To the Jews I became like a Jew, to win the Jews. To those under the law I became like one under the law (though I myself am not under the law), so as to win those under the law.

"To those not having the law I became like one

129

not having the law (though I am not free from God's law but am under Messiah's law), so as to win those not having the law. To the weak I became weak, to win the weak. I have become all things to all men so that by all possible means I might save some."

Many of the phrases Paul uses can easily be misinterpreted, distorting their meaning. They must be understood in context.

What did Paul mean by the phrase "I make myself a slave to everyone"? Does he mean that he does whatever anyone tells him to - lie, steal, kill, turn away from Yeshua? No. He does not mean that. He means that he has freely chosen to serve others, rather than just serving himself.

What did he mean by "under the law"? He equates this with being a Jew who does not know Yeshua. He means being under the authority and judgment of the Law of Moses. God commanded Israel to observe the Law of Moses, under penalty of death. The law ruled over Israel. "We were guarded by the law..." (Gal. 3:23) The Law had authority to punish transgression with death and a curse.

Messiah changed that by suffering death and becoming a curse in our place. "Messiah redeemed us from the curse of the law by becoming a curse for us, for it is written: 'Cursed is everyone who is hung on a tree.' " (Gal. 3:13) Because of that, Paul, and all Jews who have been put to death in Messiah, are no longer under the authority and judgment of the Law of Moses.

The Law of Moses was given to teach God's holiness, to show the necessity of faith, and to point to Messiah. It was not given as a means to make ourselves acceptable to God.

Paul was not looking to his own observance of

the Law to make himself righteous before God. He could only be made righteous through faith in the Lord, the same way in which Abraham was made righteous. Abraham lived 400 years before the Law was given at Sinai. He was not circumcised when God counted his faith for righteousness.

To effectively communicate the message of righteousness through faith, Paul sought to put himself in the shoes of those he sought to reach. He sought to speak from and to the position in which they found themselves before the Lord. Faith in Messiah had set Paul free from the death and curse decreed by the Law of Moses, but he knew how to convey the message to those still under the Law.

He also knew that the grace of God did not stand in opposition to the law of God. They functioned differently, but towards the same goal. "What then? Shall we sin because we are not under law but under grace? By no means! Don't you know that when you offer yourselves to someone to obey him as slaves, you are slaves to the one whom you obey —whether you are slaves to sin, which leads to death, or to obedience, which leads to righteousness?" (Rom. 6:15-16)

What did Paul mean when he said, "I became like one not having the law"? Did Paul mean that when he was with immoral Gentiles, he joined them in their immorality, i.e. "When in Rome, do as the Romans do?" Was he saying that if he were with cannibals, he would do as the cannibals do? No. He was not saying that. He would have been denying by his life the very message that he sought to communicate by his words.

He was saying, "I seek to stand on common ground with people, so that I can call them to serve the Lord according to who they are." This is what he did in Athens on Mars Hill. He spoke to the Gentile Athenians of their responsibility to their Creator. He did not speak to them of the requirements of the Law of Moses. (Acts 17:16-34)

Did he then mean, "When with Gentiles, don't be a Jew"? Of course not. No more than he meant, "When with women, don't be a man." He was not a chameleon. He knew who he was, but he also knew the nature of those he was calling to the Lord. To speak to them where they were, he put himself, as much as possible, in their place before God.

He was not without law, but he became like those who were - not in behavior, but in mindset - so that he could understand and communicate to them. That is why he said he was under Messiah's law.

What law is that? It is the two great commandments of the Law of Moses: 1. "Hear O Israel, the Lord your God, the Lord is one. And you shall love the Lord your God with all your heart, and with all your soul, and with all your strength." (Dt.6:4-5) 2. "...love your neighbor as yourself." (Lev.19:18) Included also is their practical explanation: Don't commit adultery, and don't lust. Don't murder, and don't hate. Etc. The Law of Messiah includes the universal law of God put into every person's conscience.

The Continued Applicability of the Law of Moses
   a) Hebr. 7:11-12,18-19 "If perfection could have been attained through the Levitical priesthood (for on the basis of it the law was given to the people), why was there still need for another priest to come —one in the order of Melchizedek, not in the order of Aaron? For when there is a change of the

132

priesthood, there must also be a change of the law....

"The former regulation is set aside because it was weak and useless (for the law made nothing perfect), and a better hope is introduced, by which we draw near to God."

God said in Tanakh that Messiah would be a priest forever from the order of Melchizedek. (Ps.110) Melchizedek was not from the tribe of Levi. He met with Abraham long before Levi was born. That means that the laws governing his priesthood, i.e. that of the New Covenant, are different from the laws which God gave at Sinai regulating the Aaronic priesthood.

The priesthood of Melchizedek existed long before the Levitical, or Aaronic priesthood, came into existence. It was priesthood that served the uncircumcised as well as the circumcised, for Abraham was uncircumcised when he met with Melchizedek.

The Covenant of the Law prescribed a sacrificial system which provided atonement for the repentant lawbreaker. Each new sin required a new sacrifice. There was an ongoing need for sacrifice.

That ongoing need extended far beyond the lifetime of Aaron or any of his descendants. Aaron died and was replaced by his son Eleazar. Eleazar died and was replaced by his son Pinchas. And so it went, on and on.

Many priests offered many sacrifices to atone for many sins, but all of that did not take away the power of sin over the individual. There was an endless cycle of sin, atonement, death, sin, atonement, death... The Aaronic priesthood and its sacrifices did not have the power to break that cycle by changing the individual.

Messiah does have that power in his priesthood.

In describing the New Covenant, God promised, "I will forgive their wickedness and will remember their sins no more." (Jer. 31:34) The endless cycle will be broken.

Some people have said that because God changed the regulations governing the priesthood, all the rest of His Law was annulled. There is nothing in this text in Hebrews 7 or in any other Biblical text that says or indicates that. The text simply says that the regulations for the Aaronic priesthood did not have the power to change the nature of the lawbreakers.

God had changed the priesthood before, when He took the Levites in the place of the first-born males, and instituted the Aaronic priesthood. That did not nullify the everlasting priesthood of Melchizedek. The Covenant of the Law had defined holiness and righteousness for Israel. The priesthood served to offer atonement when Israel failed to live accordingly.

That did not nullify the holiness and righteousness that God was seeking in Israel. The Law was a means of teaching it. The two major functions of the priests were to teach God's Law and to offer sacrifices for repentant lawbreakers.

b) 1Tim. 1:8-11,15 "We know that the law is good if one uses it properly. We also know that law is made not for the righteous but for lawbreakers and rebels, the ungodly and sinful, the unholy and irreligious; for those who kill their fathers or mothers, for murderers, for adulterers and perverts, for slave traders and liars and perjurers —and for whatever else is contrary to the sound doctrine that conforms to the glorious gospel of the blessed God, which he entrusted to me...."

"Here is a trustworthy saying that deserves full acceptance: Messiah Yeshua came into the world to save sinners —of whom I am the worst."

If everyone always did what is good and right, there would be no need for an external law — Mosaic, civil, or otherwise. Because everyone does not always do what is good and right, the law is given to guide, correct, and punish.

Paul, as the worst of sinners, knew the need for the Law. That is why he says everything that is ungodly and sinful is contrary to the teaching of the gospel. Whatever is contrary to the Law is also contrary to the sound doctrine of the gospel. The Law is not contrary to the promises of God. (Gal.3:21) The Law is good.

Nor is the Law contrary to the life of the Spirit. The Law was breathed by God. His Spirit worked in men to produce it.

It is the life and deeds of the flesh, unsubmitted to God, that are contrary to the life of the Spirit. The deeds of the flesh are also contrary to the Law. "But the fruit of the Spirit is love, joy, peace, patience, kindness, goodness, faithfulness, gentleness, and self-control. Against such things there is no law." (Gal.5:22-23)

c) Rom. 13:8-10 "Owe no one anything, except to love one another, for he who loves his fellowman has fulfilled the law. The commandments, 'Do not commit adultery,' 'Do not murder,' 'Do not steal,' 'Do not covet,' and any other commandment are summed up in this one rule: 'Love your neighbor as yourself.' Love does no harm to its neighbor. Therefore love is the fulness of the law."

The Law gives practical definition to what loving

God and loving one's neighbor is. Someone who walks according to the Law will walk in love. Yeshua did. Someone who walks in love will walk according to the Law. Yeshua did. Love fulfills the Law.

The Law is not about being in bondage. It is about loving God and loving our neighbor as ourselves.

"The law of the LORD is complete, bringing the soul back. The testimony of the LORD is trustworthy, making the simple wise.

"The precepts of the LORD are upright, giving joy to the heart. The commandment of the LORD is pure, giving light to the eyes.

"The fear of the LORD is clean, enduring forever. The judgments of the LORD are true and altogether righteous.

"They are more precious than gold, than much fine gold; and sweeter than honey, and the drops from the honeycomb.

"Your servant is also warned by them; in keeping them there is great reward." (Ps. 19:7-11, vv.8-12 in Hebrew)

CONCLUSION

"So God created man in His own image, in the image of God He created him; male and female He created them." (Gen. 1:27) Adam and Eve were physically different from each other, but they were both made in the image and likeness of their Creator.

God did not make one better than the other. He simply made them different. The differences were not intended to be a source of strife. They were intended to be a source of mutual blessing. The differences enabled them to become one, and to be fruitful. Their oneness was only possible because of the God-designed differences between them.

Adam and Eve were created in holiness, set apart to God. They were created to do what was good and right. The distinction between what is right and what is wrong, between what is good and what is evil, comes from the nature of God. When man was made in the image and likeness of God, that distinction was ingrained in his very being.

Adam and Eve had some responsibilities in common. There were other responsibilities that were particular to one or the other. The differences in responsibility flowed from the differences in their created nature. Their gifts were designed for their calling. The provision of particular individual gifts and responsibilities, i.e. calling, made it possible for there to be something greater than either one of them.

God's purposes in creating Jews and Gentiles parallel His purposes in creating male and female. Adam and Eve were neither Jewish nor Gentile. For the last four thousand years, by God's design, their descendants have been either one or the other.

There is much commonality in calling, but there

are also differences. The differences were not intended to be a source of strife. They were intended to be a source of mutual blessing.

When both are faithful to God's design and purpose, something greater than either one can exist. When each fulfills those responsibilities, there can be a body of believers which grows and is fruitful. (Eph. 4:16)

Yeshua himself is the best example of what God created the Jewish people to be. He is the King of the Jews. For Jews, our relationship to Torah should be the same as his. He did not abolish the Law. He lived it.

We live in a time when God has begun the restoration of all Israel to Himself. That includes restoration to His irrevocable calling. God has not changed His purpose for the Jewish people. (Rom.11:29)

The endtime remnant of Jews is faithful to that calling, and therefore plays a catalytic role in the righteous harvest of all the earth. They "keep the commandments of God and hold to the testimony of Yeshua." (Rev.12:17) They "keep the commandments of God and the faith of Yeshua." (Rev.14:12) Next to Yeshua, they are the best example for Jewish disciples.

Torah contains the God-designed particulars of Jewish existence. Since the purpose of that design and existence remain, the particulars are still operational. The only exceptions are those that result from the differences between the Old Covenant and the New Covenant. God has delineated those differences in Tanakh.

Jews should be Jews. Gentiles should be Gentiles. "Circumcision is not what counts, nor is uncircumcision. Keeping God's commandments is what counts. Each person should remain in the calling in which God called him." (1Cor. 7:19-20) No one can improve on God's design and purpose.

Sometimes, in God's design and purpose, some Gentiles were joined to the Jewish people in a special way. In Biblical times, there were Gentiles who chose to live within Israel without becoming proselytes. Their relationship to Torah was different than that of other Gentiles. In the first century, there were God-fearing Gentiles throughout the Diaspora who joined themselves to the Jewish people, adopting some customs and practices, without becoming proselytes.

In all things, it should be the love of God that motivates us. "For Messiah's love compels us, because we are convinced that one died for all, and therefore all died. And he died for all, that those who live should no longer live for themselves but for him who died for them and was raised again." (2Cor. 5:14 -15)

Each one should live for God. "This is love for God: to obey his commandments. And His commandments are not burdensome." (1John 5:3) "The entire law is summed up in a single commandment: 'Love your neighbor as yourself.' " (Gal.5:14) The rest is commentary.